MY LIFE ON SARK

BOOK 1

SO YOU WANT TO LIVE ON SARK

CHRIS DAVIES CURTIS

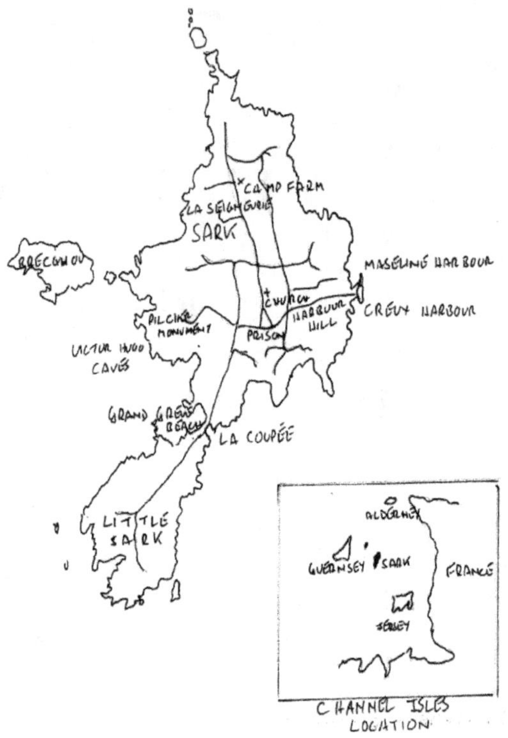

THE ISLAND OF SARK AND ITS LOCATION

****

This work is a book of memoirs based mainly on factual happenings when the author first moved to Sark. The names of some places and people have been changed.

OTHER PUBLICATIONS BY CHRIS DAVIES CURTIS

Memoirs
From a Feudal Isle to Aotearoa
From Queen's Nurse to Godzone
To Sark and Beyond

Historical
Exits and entrances

Fantasy
The Healing Hands

Romances
Nurses in Training
Nurses at Large
Nurses in New Zealand
Nurses in Retirement
The Pledge
Escape to Sark
Ellie's Story

published by Chris Curtis Books

****

Published and illustrated by the author

ISBN 978-0-473-66158-8

1

The rolling and pitching of the overnight ferry made me wonder why people paid money to thrill-seek in fairgrounds. All they had to do was to take the overnight ferry from Weymouth to the Channel Islands.

At last Ken and I arrived at Guernsey's St Peter Port main quay in the pre-dawn light of a grey February morning. With three quarters of an hour to fill until the Sark ferry left, we looked for somewhere that might be open at six thirty in the morning.

Over a welcome cup of hot coffee in a workmen's cafe on the quay, I stared blearily at my handsome, bearded husband. He still looked his neat, slim self; dark wavy hair in place and deep brown eyes bright and wide awake. He looked more my age than nine years older. I felt twice my twenty six years. I knew my fair hair was sticky and dull, and had come unravelled from its pony tail. My spectacles were smeared, and I had forgotten to put any lipstick on my dry lips. I felt a mess.

'Oh, I hope we aren't making a big mistake!'

'Well, it's a bit late for that!' Ken stirred his coffee. "I thought this was what you really wanted; excitement and challenge you said.' He smiled at the thought of my earlier enthusiasm. "Come on, where is all that optimism?' He paused as he took a sip of coffee. "You'll be OK after a good night's sleep.'

My husband was a good sailor and had slept soundly on the reclining chairs. I, on the other hand had not slept a wink and wished I had overruled Ken's insistence that the berths were too expensive.

A little revived, we walked round to the next landing to find the Sark Ferry, and watched our suitcases and trunks being loaded. The three railway containers on the way from England with all our worldly goods, would follow later, on the cargo boat, when weather permitted. I was to be pleased that I had included two beakers, plates and sets of cutlery in our suitcases. The one container with all crockery, cutlery, carpets and bed linen was delayed by bad weather for several weeks. A situation that became all too familiar in the years to come.

With difficulty we negotiated the heaving gangplank, but I refused to go down below to the passenger cabin. I later heard it called 'the coffin'. It had no windows, and access was by a hand-over-hand runged ladder. Once down, the passengers could drink and smoke themselves to oblivion, as there was a bar at one end of the cabin, which did brisk service.

Despite his tendency to asthma, Ken decided to brave the smoke fumes below. I spent the hour-long journey on the top deck, clinging to the rail and avoiding the occasional big wave that sought to sweep me overboard, revelling in the salty tang. I did not mind as the wind blew my anorak hood back, soaking my hair and causing my spectacles to mist. Refreshed by the wind and spray, I watched the grey smudge of Sark grow larger through the increasing light. We passed the small islands of Jethou and Herm, and I could see the early light behind me painting the houses of St Peter Port in gold and crimson.

At last we arrived, and my exhilaration evaporated as I felt the hard concrete of the Sark quay under my feet. Our holidays had all been in May. The weather had been warm and the cliffs aglow with wild flowers. Now it was so different.

I looked up at the towering grey cliffs; at the churning sea below and the cruel rocks by the harbour entrance and felt a deep panic in my stomach.

'B'Jour; you'll be the new people at Camp Farm? Welcome to Sark; good to have you here.' The voice behind me was warm and friendly. I turned and met Harry, the Harbour Master for the first time, with his seaman's hat, grey beard and twinkling blue eyes, and the panic left me as my confidence returned for a little while.

2

This was not to last, as reality set in again and my volatile nature asserted itself. While I stood among the piles of boxes and cases on the quay I wondered for the hundredth time if we were not making the biggest mistake of our lives. People had run guest houses with less knowledge than ours it was true. We had visited this tiny Channel Island of Sark several times, staying in a lovely granite farmhouse on holiday, and fallen in love with the Island's natural beauty and simple way of life. To live there was going to be so different. Not just to live, I kept reminding myself, but to have the audacity to offer accommodation. We had bookings to prove it. Whether our future guests would be so keen if they had known we had no previous experience, I very much doubted. Perhaps we should have settled in our new home first, before opening, but we needed an income, it just seemed an exciting thing to do at the time.

During our annual visit the previous summer Ken and I had set out to investigate the practicability of buying or renting a place to run as a guest house. We had long talked of a family business, 'but not a guest house ... unless it was on Sark!' I used to say, thinking that possibility was safely remote.

I loved people; as a District Nurse in London I had to. I also loved cooking, but housework and cleaning left me cold. Our holiday was spent looking at available properties. There were few, officially but as with any small community word travelled and we soon had quite a list of possible places to visit. With only 500 permanent residents this tiny Island measured just three miles by one and a half miles. The terrain was quite varied. On first sight from the sea the high cliffs of the Island plateau gave a barren and windswept appearance, but as soon as the steep hill was reached from the harbour there was an altogether different aspect. A road wound up one of several wooded valleys that were tucked away from the strong winds. Wild flowers peppered slopes under sycamore, ash and alder trees. On the top of the Island elm trees bent together to meet over the dirt roads, making leafy tunnels in summer. Roads were bordered by waist high banks, covered with wildflowers.

Every field, wood, valley and cliff of this unique Feudal State was owned by someone. The division of the Island's varied acres went back 400 years to the time of Elizabeth 1st. The Queen decreed that there must be at least forty families resident at all times.

Island had at that time been divided into forty *Tenements* or freeholds, each having both good farm land and a piece of cliff or *Cotils*. Those freeholds as planned by the first *Seigneur*, Helier de Carteret in 1565, still existed. Holdings could not be split by law, even to this day. As they were often several acres, with one or two houses on them, prices were well out of our reach. So the problem of housing was usually solved by taking a long lease at ground rent, and building a new house. These were more within our pocket, but none was suitable.

We followed any lead. There was the old farm house that we felt had possibilities, until we found a stream running under the kitchen floor. There was the lovely, but isolated and finally too expensive, converted barracks.

A visit to a local character who knew most of the Island's business was an idea recommended to us. He was a retired accountant and the room he showed us into was piled from floor to ceiling with ledgers and papers. Sweeping clear areas for us to sit, he produced huge tumblers of potent homemade wine. 'If you see a place you like, knock on the door and ask if they would like to sell.' He took a swig from his tumbler, while I made a tentative sip at mine, nearly choking.

'Now there is a nice place in the north of the Island. Made of stone and has a lovely garden,' he grinned at us. 'Make a nice big guest house. There's only an old lady living in it.' Our hopes rose for a moment, and then we realised he was talking about the *Seigneurie*; the home of the legendary *Dame of Sark* and current ruler of the Island.

We decided to go ahead with a property in one of the wooded valleys, which still had part of an ancient monastery in its garden. The only drawback being, it was on an annual rent. Having done our homework and realising we could afford this cottage, it only remained to see the owner who had been away. 'Sorry,' he said, but did not look it. 'No way will I let it be used for *P.G's;* even less will I let it be used to house old people brought into the island for the purpose!' This last shot floored me, until I realised the power and inaccuracy of local gossip. Knowing I was a Nurse, it was assumed I was opening an old people's home.

All our eggs having been completely shattered, and with just two days to go of our holiday, we decided to look at a property called 'Camp Farm.'

This was an unusual freehold, in that it was a small two acre holding, but was not one of the Tenements.

Some time in the distant past it had been split from the main holding.

The bungalow was solid, built of cedar shingles just after the Second World War, by the couple who were now selling. Locals assured us that it had been run as a guest house in the past, but it looked so small.

As we approached, there was a golden glow on the wooden shingled walls and roof, and sun reflected from the windows. Flowers added a bright note in the front bed, and tree lupins bushed at the side of the large lawn. A huge hydrangea grew by a conservatory attached at one side. As we neared the large enclosed front porch, the house looked settled comfortably in the surrounding lawns and hedges.

It was much bigger than it seemed. Two large bedrooms in the front, and two at the back; a long narrow kitchen; lounge; and a storeroom with a sloping roof, that we could use as a bedroom in the summer. Then there was the long conservatory that had been used as a dining room; the big front porch, and a walk-in pantry. There was even an inside toilet and bathroom, by no means standard on the Island in 1965.

It was just possible. Tentatively we made an offer, ignoring the fact that we had to persuade Ken's father to transfer his personal loan from our London home to this, as yet, un-mentioned project. Our offer was accepted.

Dazed, we returned to London at the end of the week; Ken to his advertising job and me to my District Nursing.

3

The cold light of reason returned as we settled into our London home again, but the magic and excitement remained. I tasted with loathing the car fumes and craved the sweet honey tang of gorse in bloom. As I walked the streets while visiting my patients, I found myself craning my neck to look at the remote sky. I longed for the broad horizons and billowing clouds of the Islands.

Although Ken's parents were sad that we wanted to leave London, our alternative of distant New Zealand, was a deciding factor in our favour. Ken's father, bless him, transferred his loan on our London house, but we still had to sell that to find the remainder of the purchase price. Of course we hit one of the country's financial crises, but we were fortunate finally to find a buyer. We barely made the shortfall to finalise on Camp Farm within the six months specified by Sark law.

The panic set in, then. I could barely remember how many rooms there were. What colour were the walls, inside? I had a sinking feeling that it was all cream and green. After years of working in hospitals, they were not my favourite colours.

As I looked at our silver Italian brocade curtains and thick grey fitted carpet I realised we would have some redecorating to do. The decision of what to take and what to leave nearly caused the first of many arguments. We did however have a stroke of luck when buying bed linen. A large store had had a fire and was selling top quality stock at half price. I would not have been so delighted, had I known then, that linen had to be ironed damp, and I would be hand-ironing everything.

We also had to decide what crockery and cutlery to purchase. We realised there would be little choice with the limited retailers on the Island of Guernsey, the nearest shopping area to Sark, so again chose and bought in London. The economically minded Ken insisted on plastic-like *Melamine* as it was virtually indestructible. Although it was very good quality and looked like china, I never really felt it was right. It did last, though.

Then there was bedding, pillows, tablecloths, pans and cooking equipment to choose, buy and pack.

Among all these arrangements and decisions, we also had to put our minds to our much needed income: guests.

With Ken's advertising experience, well worded entries in the *Lady* magazine and a half page advertisement in the Sark Tourist guide, we eventually had several bookings. We were grateful for anything, even one-nighters, not realising at this stage all the work involved.

We decided that Ken should only stay a couple of weeks, to settle in, and then he would return to London for six weeks, ending the financial year, and gaining some badly needed tax relief. I would be on my own, knowing few people, and with a house I could hardly remember on a remote island, with no cars and whose main means of transport was the horse and cart. No wonder I was panicking.

4

That there were no cars on Sark seemed a quirky eccentricity when we were on holiday, but arriving on that bleak February morning drove home to us how used we were to modern civilisation. How were we and our luggage to get to Camp Farm?

The carter Jim was waiting on the quay, with tractor and a rather dilapidated trailer. He was to transport anything that was delivered to the Sark quay for us, including the guests' luggage. 'Hop on,' he said. It seemed it was usual to hitch a lift up the steep Harbour Hill, although it was illegal to carry more than one person beyond the top.

I found no difficulty climbing aboard, as I had been brought up in the country, but I was glad I had worn trousers. With a roar at full throttle, Jim set off, and we realised where he had spent the previous half hour. We were to learn that the pub at the top of the hill was one of Jim's favourite drinking places. I seldom saw him sober, and he gave us many an anxious time, hoping he had remembered to collect guests' luggage. He never let us down.

'There y'are,' he said as he skidded to a halt by the pub. 'Can't take ye any further. I'll drop the cases later.' At our offer of payment, his full black beard quivered. 'That's awright; that's awright. See ye later.' He disappeared again into the public bar.

I was glad I took my overnight bag with me. His 'later' certainly was. We walked and walked. I began to realise that such a small Island can seem much larger when you are on foot. We found the dirt roads were muddy from rain. In the summer when we had been here before, it was dusty. There being no cars on Sark, and many horses, tar seal was not used. We both decided to buy good waterproof boots and bicycles, as soon as possible.

The watery, windy but intoxicating air sustained us until we finally arrived at Camp Farm. My worry about not having a key was groundless, as the front door was already open. I never did find a key to either front or back door. Few people ever locked their doors. The Morris' answered our call of 'Hello!' They rushed from the kitchen to greet us, looking the typical guest house proprietors, Muriel with cosy ample figure and grey permed hair, and Bud with clipped moustache and military bearing.

'Welcome, welcome!' Muriel had lit the fire and the kettle was boiling. Wise in the ways of the Island, she also lent us a few cups and plates. 'Now I baked you a few rock cakes, here, and we will leave you in peace, my dears.' Muriel's kindness nearly brought on the tears, but I managed to thank her.

Sustained by tea and cake, Ken and I had our first real look at our new home. What I saw horrified me. First there was the kitchen. No nice electric cooker. I would have to learn to cook on a solid fuel Rayburn range that looked as if it had come out of the Ark. I named it 'the Monstrosity' there and then. My mind recoiled with horror at the thought of our future guests expecting the good home cooking, advertised in our brochure. I felt the sooner the Rayburn went the better. In fact in time I learned almost to love the thing. Its pastry was always a rich golden brown all over, and the meat tender and juicy.

The only windows in the kitchen opened to the sun lounge, which had obviously been added later. They would prove very convenient for serving guests when we used the sun lounge as dining room, but it made the kitchen so dark.

A stone 'Butler' sink faced a blank wall. The overall cream and green gloss paintwork, confirmed my earlier memories of Hospital decor, as did the green and cream lino tiles.

We continued our tour, becoming more and more depressed. We had bought a few beds, chairs and a table with the property but without the touches of everyday living, the place was soulless. As we wandered from room to room, we suddenly heard a whistling shriek from the front of the house.

'What on earth was that?' Ken walked to the large enclosed front porch. 'Look the wind coming through that keyhole and straight through the other door!' He said pointing to the open keyhole, where the force six gale was whistling through. 'That needs blocking up.' We were never able to silence the noise until we re-built the porch and faced the door in a different direction.

As Ken stood by the doorway, a thin stream of water suddenly dripped on his head, and trickled through his beard. He stepped back hurriedly, wiping water out of his eyes. 'Grab a bucket or something, will you, Chris?' He exclaimed. We discovered that when the porch was added, the gutter was left to run through the ceiling. When it rained hard it could not cope with the added water flow and the bucket was a permanent fixture until the porch was rebuilt.

In silence we prepared an evening meal and decided that the best place to sleep that night was in the warm kitchen.

Pulling our mattress onto the floor in front of the Rayburn, I suddenly found my sense of adventure returning.

'Come on, Ken,' I said, 'This is a bit like camping with your scouts; well it is called *Camp Farm* after all!'

<h1 style="text-align:center">5</h1>

-

Next morning was bright and crisp; the storm only a memory. I was to discover this rapid change of weather peculiar to Island life, and it was one of the things I learned to love.

Refreshed and encouraged by a good night's sleep (I think I would have slept on the hard floor without the mattress) we explored our two and a half acres independently. Ken wanted to walk the boundaries, while I needed just to soak up the sunshine.

The large front lawn had overgrown flower borders at either side. It looked huge and stretched right to the long front Veronica hedge, with a small gate in the middle which separated us from the road. On that clear day I could see right over the sparkling sea to the smaller Islands of Herm and Jetou that we had passed the previous day. On the far horizon was the large Island of Guernsey, looking deceptively close in the crisp air.

The land was prime for growing, provided you did not try anything higher than the banks and hedges. Salt winds burned everything that crept above.

That did not concern me on our first day. Taking a deep breath of the intoxicating, gorse perfumed air I flung myself full length on the back lawn. Grabbing tufts of grass in each hand I flung them high. 'It's ours at last; we have our little bit of Sark!' I shouted. I stood up suddenly as I heard a tractor in the next field, and blushed as I saw who was driving it. We had met Hap at the old farmhouse when we were on holiday, as he was friends with the owners.

He waved and grinned at me, so I made a 'cup of tea drinking' gesture, and he cut the engine, climbing over the bank. '*Buggre!*' He laughed as he looked at the tufts of grass. I was used by now to his favourite Patois expression. '*Buggre* me, I thought you were ploughing by hand, eh?'

Hap was our first visitor. I did not realise at the time he and his family were to be interwoven with my life on Sark for many years to come.

He was a typical Sarkese, as the indigenous residents were called. His stocky appearance, ruddy face and thick Gallic accent showed his ancestry from Normandy, as did his Patois. I delighted in his wicked sense of humour and we later developed a rapport that was unusual between the Sark and English residents. For all his joking, he was a gentleman.

He always took his hat off when he came into the kitchen, showing the two-tone brow of sunburn and baby pink. That visit was the first of many. I used to call out as he helped us in our fields or worked in neighbouring ones, 'do you want a wet, Hap?' Much to the bemusement of anyone overhearing.

Later that day our luggage finally arrived, and I was glad of the borrowed cups and those I had packed. All that day and the next we had a stream of visitors. February on Sark is at the end of an isolated winter and new residents are a source of general interest. Harry's wife was one of the first to arrive. 'Hi,' she called through the open back door. 'You met my husband yesterday;

he's Harbour Master. I guess you could use a few eggs?' I thought the accent was American or Canadian. I invited her in and soon made a cup of coffee from the constantly simmering, solid bottomed kettle on the Rayburn hotplate.

'It's great to have fresh blood! A lot of the 'ex colonials' ... the *lower cocktail set* ... go to the Canary Islands or Spain for most of the winter.' She took a sip of coffee, 'we get bored with the same old faces.'

'What do you mean by *lower cocktail set*?'

She laughed. 'Well, there are really four social groups here. You can call them classes, if you like,' she shrugged. 'There is the Dame and the very wealthy. They tend to socialise together; they are the *upper cocktail set*. There are the *lower cocktail set* who also have their own little group.' She drained her cup. 'Then there are the *working English*, like you and me ... well I'm Canadian; and the *Sarkese*, who keep themselves to themselves.'

'Goodness, it sounds complicated. Do you mean they keep in their, er, groups?'

'Well, mostly. I am married to a *Sarkese*, so I run foul of both the *Sarkese* and the English.' She said it with a flippant tone, but I noted a sadness. I liked Sue's openness, and as I waved good bye, hoped I had made my first female Sark friend.

6

A few days later, two of our railway containers arrived from England. The cargo boat from Southampton was apparently too full to carry all three, so the third one would arrive as soon as there was room. Fortunately we had been advised to book the smaller 'A' size British rail containers, as these were the only size that would pass through the tunnel at the Sark harbour. This long tunnel had been hacked through a rocky outcrop when the New 'Maseline' harbour was built just after the Second World War and was higher than that from the Old 'Creux' harbour, which was mostly used by Sark's fishermen. This picturesque original harbour was shallow, and dry at low tide, but sometimes used if the wind made it difficult for passenger boats to enter the other harbour. We later heard stories of less well advised people having to unpack everything and have it carted piecemeal up the steep Harbour hill by trailer.

Anxiously we awaited the last container. 'Not to worry.' We were told. 'It will come on the next cargo boat. Next week, probably.' We had planned to get as much unpacking and sorting underway before Ken had to return to London.

Nothing could be done until the last container arrived. It held the carpets, curtains, crockery and cutlery, of course!

The winds started to blow again in the night, and we had to learn our first lesson of patience. If the wind blew strongly Northeast into the deep water Maseline Harbour, no boats could berth there, as the sea eddied into the confined inlet, making it impossible to tie up to the quay. In a high tide it was possible for boats to negotiate the narrow entrance into Creux harbour, on the other side of the harbour hill. If the tide was low, and Creux just a muddy inlet, there was no way to receive supplies or get off the Island. We soon learned to listen attentively to weather forecasts, particularly if expecting guests or planning a trip. If bad weather or a strong wind was forecast, a change of plans was imperative, and an earlier boat caught before the weather closed in.

Sark's three small general groceries, bakery, butcher and haberdashery supplied everyday needs, but there were several items we needed in Guernsey, the nearest large island and boasting a good shopping centre.

We also needed to arrange supplies from a wholesaler for the start of the visitors' season. We had been told of one that most guest house owners used. Discount was offered for cleaning and baking needs, as well as some hardware items. First we needed to enrol on their list and then to see what was available.

A few days before Ken left, the winds abated, but the sea was still very rough. I had never been a good sailor, but needs must, so we made a trip over to St Peter Port, Guernsey's main town. Over the years I learned to fix my eyes on the rolling horizon, and as long as I did not have to talk to anyone, managed to retain my breakfast. When I discovered the Homeopathic 'Bach Rescue Remedy' drops, all seasickness was well under control. I hated to take seasick pills as I was like a zombie for the rest of the day. Surprisingly several residents seldom left the Island unless the sea was calm and with little wind. Some locals had not left in years.

Once on Guernsey, we hired a car to reach the wholesaler as it was on the other side of the Island. After enrolling with the company for the first time, hiring a car was civilised. We just telephoned the hire company, gave our names and the time of boat we were catching.

On arrival at the Guernsey quay a car would be there with the hirer's name on a piece of cardboard in the window. The keys were lodged above the visor. On return a cheque and the keys were left in the same place. I never heard of any being stolen, though one was shipped to the mainland by mistake. It had been parked in the wrong area, where cars were transported over to Southampton. I understand the hiring company was less than pleased. The hirer was told that if he did it again, he would have to go over and collect it at his own cost.

It was a sunny day, and we enjoyed a tour of the larger Island as we sought the wholesaler, getting thoroughly lost in the winding, high banked country lanes. We were surprised at the extensive building on all roads. There was little open countryside. Much of the land was covered with glasshouses, as tomato and freesia growing were the main horticultural industries. Many houses and farms were built of attractive granite in tones of grey, blue-grey and pink. Gardens, more sheltered than those on Sark, were ablaze with yellow Forsythia, pink Camellias and early spring flowers.

After we finally located the wholesale company and received their supplies list, we drove back to St Peter Port and returned the car. Separating, we agreed to meet up at the Sark quay, half an hour before the boat sailed. I wanted to look at table linen and explore the many shops. Ken said he had something he had to do; in any case he hated wandering round shops, like most men.

I became a little anxious as my usually punctual husband arrived back with only a few minutes to spare. As he helped me with the various packets, I noticed a large bulge in his Army Surplus Duffle coat pocket. As he sat heavily next to me, a little black nose peeped out followed by a silvery head.

'Ken, what on earth ... ?'

'Well, I thought you might be lonely with me gone.' '

Oh, he's a darling. What shall we call him?' I asked as I cuddled the tiny puppy. We spent the trip thinking of names and finally decided on 'Hugo' after the writer, Victor Hugo who had spent many years in the Islands.

I had no premonition then, that this tiny scrap would grow to be a large and unruly Labrador. It took him three years to outgrow puppyhood, and wore my nerves to shreds on our first few years on Sark.

Many were the telephone calls from people with slightly hysterical voices beseeching us to collect our well meaning but misguided pup. He felt it his duty to help in all activities, especially with such exciting things as mixing concrete or mucking out stables. Later he was one of the biggest attractions for our guests. Those returning would ask on arrival 'Where's Hugo?' before they were hardly in the door.

The two weeks of Ken's stay went quickly. Rooms that had carpet could be arranged, but the lounge furniture was piled in one corner awaiting the missing railway container. This of course arrived a week after he left.

It was with a little resentment that I saw Ken depart from the tiny Maseline Harbour, a few days later. I thought of all the decorating to be done. With only four years of marriage, I felt he left too readily. Whatever else he was, I realised my stoical husband was not romantic.

7

The third furniture container arrived at last. It was delivered by Bruce. He was the main carter for larger items. He was a fisherman with his brother Dave, and also an authority on small farming. In the many years I was to know him, Bruce was always the same. Smiling and cheerful, his weather beaten face and stocky body were a welcome and reassuring sight. In the early days he had a shyness to us that was almost deferential, and I was delighted when he first called me by my Christian name. This attitude was common to most Sarkese. They were a proud, insular people, and most families could trace their ancestry to ancient Normandy stock. Their Patois had evolved from pure Norman French. Although I could speak reasonable French, I never could understand it.

The Sarkese' acceptance of the British residents bordered on mere tolerance. Any high-handed treatment often had swift retribution. Hap told me of a particular ex-colonial resident who stopped a local woman taking a short cut through his fields. She consequently missed the boat.

'What happened? Did the family complain?'

'Well no, not exactly,' he looked innocently at me.

'It was bad luck that the next day when they were unloading his laundry, it fell into the harbour, eh?'

As we were working English and I was a Nurse, I think we were accepted as possible useful additions to the Island. Whatever the reason I had no shortage of helpers to unload the furniture; place it where needed and lay the carpet while Ken was away. I had so many visitors and invitations, that I was hard put to find time to paint the kitchen and lounge. Nevertheless, eventually it was almost finished. With walls of brilliant white and yellow cupboards, the kitchen took on a new lease of life. Our Italian brocade curtains set off the newly painted silver grey and blush pink lounge, and a Persian-type rug in front of the fireplace added a luxurious touch.

Wishing to show off my new home, I invited a few lady friends for a tea by the lounge fire. Although it was March by then, and a little warmer, I was glad of the Rayburn and open fire. I had almost mastered the monstrosity and produced passable scones and fairy cakes. My visitors settled in the lounge, I went to top up the kettle, but there was no water in the tap! We had a borehole and an underground rainwater tank; I could not believe they were dry.

Then I realised that the ancient pump had finally burned out, and the header tank was empty. With the Rayburn at full blast I had visions of the hot water tank exploding like a bomb.

I popped my head round the lounge door. 'Excuse me ladies, I have a little problem.' I produced as many spades and shovels as I could find. 'I have invented a new party game!' Among giggles and coughs, we transferred all the live coals from stove to open fireplace. It was not until later I learned that the hot water tank had a safety valve and could not empty. I expect it caused some hilarity round the Island when the story was told.

I realised I had much to learn, but the early worries dissolved as the days became longer. There was the smell of spring everywhere, and I could hear the first lambs in a field behind the house. Daffodils and Irises had pushed through the edge of the lawn and were in flower. Even the winds were less cold, but showers were swift and heavy. As we relied on rain for our water supply, even that was a blessing. I knew we were doing the right thing, and was looking forward to our first guests' arrival, just before Easter.

Ken was due back then and it was clear in his phone calls that he was keen to start life on Sark. He was a good gardener and hoped to grow enough vegetables to supply the guest house and wanted to get the first crop in the ground.

As the fine spring weather warmed the earth, I thought I would plant the first few vegetables. The soil was rich and dark, and it was a joy to be outside. The rows were neat, and marked with sticks at each end, with string tied to each to ward off birds.

Feeling rather pleased with myself, the next day I decided to mow the large front lawn. We had bought an ancient petrol roller mower from the Morris'. It started well, to my surprise, and sailed down the full length of the lawn. As I approached the flowerbed near the road I tried to disengage the gear by the handle; it was stuck. The heavy roller carried on over the flower bed, stalling only when it hit the bank. As I sank down on the grass, not sure whether to laugh or cry, there was a yap behind me. It was Hugo looking so pleased with himself, with a stick in his mouth ... attached to string and other sticks. My vegetable markers!

Gradually a pattern emerged from my first days of seeming muddle. Ken was due back at Easter, but our first guests were arriving a week before he returned.

It was a family from Holland; a couple with a child of seven. They were staying for two weeks, so I hoped they would be alright, and that I would cope on my own.

Jeanne, Pieter and young Jos Vaasson were the perfect first guests. Jeanne was not much older than me, and we developed a rapport. I was impressed with their command of English. Jos adored Hugo, now all wagging tail and huge paws as they romped on the front lawn. Pieter was a reporter and we could not have had better free publicity. When they returned home he wrote a delightful article about Sark, and Camp Farm. For years we had people booking on the strength of Pieter's words.

Ken arrived, and seemed pleased with all the progress I had made and settled into his new life.

Over the past few weeks I had also seen some of the residents returning, after wintering in exotic places. With them came the new Doctor. The previous one was retiring, and Dr Henry King would be the only medical practitioner for the five hundred residents and many visitors.

There was no other Doctor, vet or nurse on Sark, and Dr King was also the Medical Officer of Health. It was a big responsibility, and a lonely post. I had decided to offer my services as district nurse in a private and limited way but did not want to tread on anyone's toes. I was sure someone would have been practicing and discovered that a retired nurse had helped the previous doctor on occasion. I went to see her.

'You do what you like, my dear.' I was not sure how genuine this was. As I left, she said, casually. 'You have been to see La Dame, of course?'

The legendry Dame of Sark, Sybil Hathaway, was the undisputed head of the Island, though it was governed by its own *Chief Pleas*.

This parliament consisted of the forty *tenement* owners, and twelve *deputies* elected by the non-tenement Sark residents. There were also several supervising officers and two elected *constables*. While she only had a casting vote in *Chief Pleas,* La Dame had her finger on Sark's pulse and liked to know all of its happenings. Any problems were taken to her, and she was respected throughout the Island. She was a formidable personality, despite her age of over eighty. The thought of visiting *La Seigneurie*, her home, turned my knees to jelly. Well, I told myself, she could not be worse than a few Matrons I knew.

I phoned and made an appointment, and was invited to tea, much to my surprise. Most newcomers were vetted soon after arrival. I was shown into a beautifully furnished small sitting room where a fire was blazing. On a low table a bone china and silver service was ready. Dame Sybil Hathaway's appearance did not dispel my first thoughts of her likeness to a hospital matron. I could easily imagine her in starched cap and severe uniform, but I could see she had been beautiful; was still handsome with her waving white hair and bright eyes behind spectacles. A firm jaw brought to mind the many tales I had read of her determination during the occupation of Sark in the Second World War.

There were many stories of how she prevented the Germans from making life totally unbearable on the Island. Tea was poured into the fragile cups and I tried to eat a sandwich, feeling a little nervous and hoping I did not drop crumbs onto the expensive-looking Persian carpet.

'So you are Christine Davies; you and your husband have bought Camp Farm, I hear.'

'Yes, Marm.' (How *did* you address her?)

'I gather you want to be a District Nurse here?' She picked up a letter. 'Well, I have been forewarned, though I would like to have heard from you first.' She looked over her spectacles at me. 'You were a nurse in London, I hear. They thought highly of you at the Queen's Institute.'

Keen to everything by the book, I had written to the Queen's Institute of District Nursing to ask what fees I should charge, and if it was in order for me to wear my old nursing uniform, which I had been given. Apparently the Institute had written promptly to Dame Sybil, saying how pleased they were that there would be a District Nurse on Sark at last, as they assumed I had been appointed by the Island.

'Well, I am sure the English residents will be glad of your help. I doubt if you will have any Sarkese patients, Mrs Davies.' She stood up. 'I hope you enjoy your time here, however long it may be.' I was dismissed.

In the event, La Dame was to be proved wrong. As both Dr King and I were new to the Island we soon built a rapport, and he seemed pleased to use my services. I suspect he felt the medical isolation acutely, as he often discussed patients with me. Unfortunately, he left after only a year to join a larger practice in England.

My first case was not one to be sought, and came only because the other nurse was away. The call came just as I was falling asleep after a tiring day.

'Is that the nurse? Doctor said to ring. Can you come and see to mother, please?' The voice was hesitant. 'The undertaker can't get over till tomorrow. I'll send a tractor for you. I have special permission from the Constable.' I could hardly say 'No' and was grateful that I would not be trying to find the house in the dark on my bicycle. Normally no tractors were allowed out after ten at night without special permission.

Shivering, I changed back into thick trousers and sweater, boots and waterproof jacket, leaving Ken cosily warm in bed. A draughty trip on the step of a tractor, made me suitably subdued, but death had no worries for me. I gently washed the old Sark grandmother, dressing her in a special nightdress kept for the occasion. Popping in her false teeth and tucking a pillow under her jaw, to stop her mouth gaping, I straightening her arms. She looked so peaceful. I had a certain satisfaction of realising La Dame was not always right.

I did not push myself as a nurse. For one thing I had quite enough to do in the Guest House. I was also aware that we were being watched and assessed. It was a new experience to be an immigrant, and my heart went out to those West Indians and Greek Cypriots recently my patients in London.

9

Hap was our friend from the start. While he treated Ken as 'man to man', he and I had a unique relationship. Most Sarkese treated us with a varying degree of reserve, waiting for us to prove ourselves, or to give up when the going got too tough. Hap, on the other hand delighted in baiting me, toning down not at all his usual picturesque language. When he found I responded in kind, a friendly war existed between us. His family at first seemed alarmed, but when they realised it fell short of blows, became accustomed to it. I told them, when I knew them well, that the day Hap was polite to me and I to him, then they should start worrying.

We had been on Sark for a couple of months when Hap called in for his usual 'wet' and a piece of homemade cake. He was unusually reserved.

'What is it, Hap? Is the cake that bad?'

'No it's OK for an English cook. Look, you said you want to do some nursing.' He took a huge bite. 'Well, it's my daughter Annie. She's expecting her third and won't go to Guernsey to have it, eh?'

He licked the crumbs off his fingers and gave a small belch. 'S'cuse; she had the other two here. No problem. Well, will you go and see her?'

'Er, well, yes, but ... ,'

'Good, that's settled then.' He was gone before I could say anything more.

Next day found me visiting the general store the family ran. Annie was behind the counter looking as if the baby was due any minute. I was invited in for a cup of tea while May, her mother took over the shop.

'S'good of you to help. Dad said you will try to persuade Dr King to let me stay. Well I'm not going to Guernsey anyway. I'll deliver it myself if I have to!'

I could see she meant it; so I went to see the Doctor.

'I'm not a midwife, Doctor. In fact I've never seen a baby born.' He looked surprised. 'We had emergency lessons on the district, but in London there were enough Midwives. We did do some post natals, of course.'

'You think she means it; that she won't go over anyway?'

'I think so. Hap says she's very stubborn.'

We agreed that I would set up the bedroom; at least I knew how to do that. The family would call us both in when the baby started to come and Dr King would do the delivery. It seemed simple enough.

For the next couple of weeks I read my 'Textbook for Midwives' avidly. Together, Annie and I prepared the room with hot water bottle ready in the cot, waterproof sheets, towels and newspapers piled to one side; and a neat stack of tiny baby clothes in the cupboard. This was long before pre-packaged dressings. On the district in London I had learned how to roll cotton wool balls and fold gauze squares to be sterilized in metal biscuit tins in the oven. I prepared dressings, cotton wool, sani-pad and chord ties; there were no shortages of tins from the shop.

All I would have to do was wash baby and mother afterwards, or so I thought.

A few days before our fifth wedding anniversary on nineteenth of May, Annie's husband, Sam, rang at two in the morning.

'I think it's on the way, nurse. I've rung Dr.'

Relieved that we only had a few guests, I told a sleepy husband what to do for their breakfast.

I had by then a general permit from the constables to ride on a tractor runway for night calls, so Sam collected me, and I decided to hitch my bicycle on the link box at the back as I had no idea how long I would be. It was one of the family farm tractors, so I thought it may not be available when I needed to return.

Dr King was there when I arrived.

'She's quite a way to go. Call me when the waters break.'

I looked at Annie and hoped to goodness she would know, as I certainly did not.

The contractions were not too frequent at this stage, and we chatted for a while. A half hour elapsed and it looked to me as if the contractions were much more frequent. Annie started to grunt a little each time, gripping the bedpost.

'Chris, I think it is coming! I want to push.'

'God, it can't be yet. You had better pant; yes that's what the book said. Pant. Let me have a look.'

What I saw sent me shooting into the kitchen to Sam.

'Quick; phone Dr King. It's on the way.' Unbeknown to us he had just gone out on another emergency.

I took another look. Sure enough that looked like the top of the baby's head. I mentally revised the chapter on delivery techniques. 'Push the head so it is not delivered at contraction; feel for the chord round the baby's neck; when the head is delivered wipe baby's eyes with moist cotton wool and clear the mouth; deliver the upper shoulder and then the lower one, and the baby just slides out.' And that is exactly what happened.

It was all over so quickly and easily, that I was tying the chord ties before I realised I had done my first delivery.

My knees were shaking as I walked in to the kitchen.

'Congratulations, you have a lovely little daughter.' I was just saying to Sam as Dr King walked in.

'Oh, my God, I am so sorry. I came as quickly as I could.' We went together into the bedroom, and I was glad he attended to the after birth, as I had been a bit worried about how to do that.

We wetted the new baby's head after I had settled mother and baby, and I cycled home weary but elated.

I did not realise at the time, but that morning's work was as good as ten years residency in establishing us on Sark.

10

In my daily visits to mother and baby I got to know the two younger children Jerry and Louise. They were shy at first, but soon became used to me and helped their mother and new little sister, Valerie. Everyone in that family was busy. Hap's wife, May worked in the shop and helped bring up the family; Sam, Annie's husband had a farm to run. My admiration for these people grew as I knew them better. With no National Health Service, unemployment benefit or pension, the old system of everyone doing their bit in the extended family really worked. An extended family it certainly was too, as there were five generations alive and living on Sark at that time.

Ken and I were to have the privilege to meet them all a few weeks after little Valerie's birth. It was Hap again who was sent as ambassador.

'Annie and Sam have asked me to ask you; well if you would ... '

'Come on Hap, spit it out!'

'Would you be agreeable to be one of little Val's godparents. You may not want to; we would understand, eh?

I was speechless. It was almost unheard of for an English person to be godparent to a Sark child.

'Hap, I would be delighted.'

It was at the party afterwards that we met the rest of the large family, though I could not remember all their names even years afterwards.

This was the beginning of our association with the family. Many, many times we were repaid for my small service. As our smallholding began and expanded, Sam became one of our chief advisors. As we grew more and more vegetables, so Hap helped with the tractor work. Not without recompense, as I was quick to point out to him. He must have drunk gallons of tea and eaten mountains of cake, which of course he maintained was a chore in itself.

As if I had passed a test, more nursing cases came my way that first year. Soon after the delivery, I had a phone call from the Doctor.

'I wonder if you can help. A Sark lady, Mrs Jacks, has had a stroke; she has a hemiplegia and I think she should go on the ambulance launch to the hospital in Guernsey.' I could hear his sigh.

'She refuses to go. I have to see someone else; see what you can do will you?'

The two man emergency team was standing by and the lady in question was already in the ambulance caravan, ready to be towed by tractor. The ruling that there were no cars on Sark, extended to ambulance and fire engine. In this case a caravan had been converted with all the necessary first aid equipment; but it had to be pulled by a tractor.

'No! No! I not go. Home.' Mrs Jacks mumbled from stiff lips.

Victor, the voluntary ambulance attendant, was used to emergency care. He had been a medical orderly in the war, and was the mainstay of the Sark Ambulance for many years, but even he could not persuade her.

'Does she have a husband, Victor? Yes? Well where is he; can someone go and get him, please?' I thought it strange he was not there and should have been warned by Victor's elbow jabbing my ribs.

Mr Jacks soon arrived. He was surprisingly neat and well dressed, with a small moustache, while his wife in contrast was untidy and unkempt.

As soon as my patient saw her husband, she went red in the face; I thought she was having another stroke. He did not even try and persuade his wife; just stood and stared at her, saying nothing. She was adamant and we could not force her.

I reported to Dr King, and so we had to take her home to Little Sark over the Coupee which divided the Island almost into two; Little Sark and Great Sark. This bridge-like narrow strip of land, three hundred feet high and only one tractor width had been fenced on each side and the road made substantial as recently as the end of the last war by German prisoners. Before that it had been rough with only a light rail. I had seen pictures of people crawling from one side to the other in gale force winds, in danger of being swept to the beach below.

The journey in a swaying caravan over the high narrow causeway, with sheer drops each side, was bad enough and made me feel like a second stretcher case, as I peered through the window.

Sight of the two storey cottage did not cheer me. The bedroom was up a steep flight of stairs. 'How on earth are we to get the patient up there?' I asked Victor. The team had done this before.

Mrs Jacks was strapped into the stretcher and she was hauled up feet first. Just as we were about to lift her onto the bed, she mumbled something.

Bending down I asked her to repeat. 'Will go now; Guernsey!' I had been talking to the patient all the way. Whether it was that, or sheer bloody mindedness, she had suddenly decided that she *would* go over to the hospital in Guernsey after all. Everything was done in reverse.

As we finally saw the ambulance launch off, I turned to Victor.

'Why was the husband so unhelpful and she looked mad at him, too. You would think he would be sympathetic.'

'Not really,' Victor grinned. 'I tried to warn you. They haven't lived together or spoken for years!'

From that day I decided to listen more to local gossip.

11

The first of the spring flowers, that were the greatest adornment of the Island, had started to peep above the brown bracken and blond grasses when we arrived in February. By Easter the cliffs were brilliant with honey-scented gorse. Powdery yellow primroses, bright red Campion, white Alexanders, and a few early bluebells, painted the hedgerows. Despite all that needed to be done, Ken and I managed to enjoy a few walks, and it was good to have him with me at last to share the work and the adventure.

In the beginning we only took eight guests; two for each bedroom. With only one bathroom and toilet combined we felt it was necessary to supply a bowl and jug of hot water to each bedroom, in the morning. We both remembered the frustration of having to queue for a bathroom on our past holidays. For those who needed to get up in the night and were unable to make it to the toilet along the corridor, each room had what the Sarkese appropriately called a 'gozunder'. Later, thanks to a small legacy from an old aunt of Ken's, we installed washbasins in each room and another toilet.

Ken and I had decided in our many discussions to offer bed, breakfast and evening meal, with packed lunch as an optional extra. I balked at a cooked lunch. In any case, most people went out all day walking the cliffs or descended the steep paths to a favourite beach and did not want to come back in the middle of the day. They were our preferred people. Only very occasionally guests stayed around the house and garden all day, which we did not mind, but it seemed such a waste of a holiday.

Ken hit on a popular idea of having a self-service 'shop' in the dining room. Guests could buy crisps, chocolate bars, and slab cake in a wrapper. On request I gave small polythene bags of salad, and fruit. The children particularly liked the shop.

We started to specialise in family holidays, taking children of all ages, and bought two cots, but this brought its own problems. One of these was feeding children and adults at the same time. Eventually we gave a meal to children under four, at five in the evening, enabling parents to settle the littlies before their own dinner. It also ensured a happy dining room. We had one or two unpleasant experiences before we made this compulsory.

Older guests had stormed out of the dining room, unable to tolerate a particularly undisciplined youngster. Eventually if anyone wanted to book at the same time as there were several children staying, we made sure they knew about it.

Gradually our routine evolved. First came the early morning cup of tea. For this the monstrosity had to be stoked to boil the two large cast iron kettles that were always on the hotplate. Breakfast was staggered over an hour and kept me on my toes trying not to serve singed bacon or rubbery eggs. I learned to cook the bacon on one side, and then flip it back into a hot pan just as it was needed. I half-cooked the toast too, until we hit on the idea to put a toaster on each table. Guests were delighted to do their own and it avoided wastage.

One of the amusing and predictable reactions of guests was whether to have tea or coffee for breakfast. On arrival we checked likes, dislikes and preferences. So many times, those who had decided on tea, as soon as the wafts of fresh ground coffee permeated into the bedrooms, there would be a timid knock on the door.

'Sorry to bother you ... er; do you think we could have coffee instead of tea, please?'

I soon learned to be well organised in case of disasters. There were surprisingly few, although one or two stand out in my memory. There was the grilled mackerel with cheese topping that landed on the floor.

Having extolled this special breakfast dish to my guests I had to produce it. Fortunately I had just scrubbed the floor, so scraped up the fish and invented a new dish, making cheese and mackerel fish cakes instead. Then there was the time Hugo ran off with the joint, and I had to do a menu reorganisation.

Adaptation became our byword especially in the first few weeks. For the four years of our marriage, we had seen little of each other; now we were together all the time. We were both practical people but temperamentally were very different. Ken was slow and methodical. I, on the other hand was quick, intuitive and impetuous. We each had our jobs. Ken set tables and served; I cooked the food and did most of the housework. I was my own worst enemy as I became very impatient with Ken at times. We had a few blazing rows, until we realised the guests could hear. One of the problems was the breakfast washing up.

Once the Rayburn was stoked and hot, it was sensible to cook as much of the evening meal as was practicable. Until the dishes were safely out of the way in our long, thin kitchen we just got in each other's way. It resolved in my washing plates as they came off the tables. One less job for Ken, however there was enough for him to do outside as there were two acres of garden to look after, and vegetables to grow.

12

Once I had learned to use the solid fuel cooker, I delighted in its even cooking temperature. The oven was so deep that two baking trays could be lined together on each shelf. Using the two shelves and bottom, it was amazing how much could be cooked at one time. I became adept at 'batch baking.' Temperatures graded from top for pastry, to middle for meat and a slow cook pudding at the base.

It all depended of course on which way the wind was blowing. A strong North Easter meant a blazing hot oven, while a sluggish South West sometimes had me almost in tears as the temperature just would not increase. We bought a small four ring gas stove to supplement the two rings already in the kitchen. At least I could cook my Yorkshire puddings without fear of a soggy mess. Poring through cookery books I devised fourteen different menus. This made sure people staying longer than a week did not have too many duplicates. I gave a cooked pudding at the beginning of the holiday season, as the weather was not so hot.

My intention to revert to a cold sweet never materialised as many of my invented sweets were very popular. One was an accident, born of a very dry batch of slab cake intended for the 'shop,' but an invented recipe proved a good standby for using stale cake and biscuits. Crumbling the cake into an ovenproof dish and mixing it with two egg yolks and a little milk, it was baked in a slow oven. Next came a layer of cooked apple, plums or any tart fruit. The egg whites were made into a meringue.

Another recipe, that was popular when we later had an abundance of goat's milk and eggs, used any stale bread. Half a pint of milk, one ounce of butter, one ounce of sugar (I preferred soft brown) and a good ounce of cocoa were slowly brought to the boil. This was poured on to a dish of crumbled stale bread. Two egg yolks were whisked into this and the whole baked until set. The result was like a chocolate sponge. Again fruit could be layered before a meringue was made with the egg whites, again.

Some sweets I made from an adaptation of cake recipes. A rich gingerbread with custard or cold with bottled pears and cream was popular. An eggless chocolate cake that was a childhood favourite was delicious cooked over a base of tinned apricots.

My 'Lemon Surprise' was appropriately named as it never turned out the same. Cooked in a water bath it depended on the proportion of milk and lemon juice, and how well the monstrosity was behaving. Sometimes it separated out to a type of lemon curd at the base, and at others it was more watery. Either way it was delicious. About three ounces of butter were beaten with five ounces of soft brown sugar and two egg yolks were added; then the juice of two to three lemons, along with the grated peel. Next four ounces of self raising flour and half a pint of milk were folded in. Lastly two well beaten egg whites were also folded in and the mix placed in a dish which rested in a larger one with water, as a water bath. The cooking took about an hour at a fairly hot temperature. All these sweets were accompanied by rich, buttercup yellow Sark cream. Separated from the Guernsey cows' milk, the cream and butter made normal types insipid by comparison.

As there was no temperature gauge on the oven door I had to become adept at discovering if the temperature was right. After a few disasters I was able to assess accurately. When guests begged a recipe, I was rather vague, as indeed with the quantities. I suppose I was called an intuitive cook. If it looked right and tasted good, I was satisfied.

The main course was more straight-forward but also allowed for some imagination. Standard joints of beef, leg and shoulder of lamb and 'hand' (a shoulder cut) or leg of pork could be embellished with herbs and stuffing. Additions of a subtle smear of garlic and sprinkling of soy sauce went undetected by the fussiest guest and added an exotic touch.

Much of the beef was from the Guernsey cattle, and not generally accepted as suitable for the table. As with the milk and cream the fat was a bright golden yellow. Many butchers regarded it as second class quality and it could be tough; after all it had been free ranging all the year. When cooked in a slow oven, and surrounded by vegetables that were liquidised to make a thick gravy, this beef was much enjoyed by my guests, and many were the requested second helpings.

To vary from the traditional joint, I made a steak and kidney pie or a dish I named 'London Beef Bake.' In both cases the meat was cooked slowly in the oven.

For the 'Bake' a savoury herb scone mix was rolled in balls in toasted bread crumbs, and dropped on top of the hot meat about three quarters of an hour before needed.

It was not long before I became used to the preparation of meals and was able to get out of the kitchen occasionally, and spend more time getting to know our guests. Ken, as server in the dining room was able to chat

freely with them, while most of my communication had
been with my head stuck through the window between
kitchen and dining room.

13

Although we had some bookings for the first year, there were vacancies in the off-peak months. We had to rely in part on word-of-mouth recommendations from the established guest houses and people in the village. My involvement with Hap's family was a great bonus.

Several 'casuals' came our way, but we found that people staying one night gave substantial work for very little return. Many of these were in the 'let's see what this peculiar little Island is like' category; this included the majority of French visitors. Often, they would arrive without booking and yet still expect accommodation. After our first year we learned our lesson.

'I've got four French in the shop,' phoned Annie, one day. 'They want a night's stay. Could you take them? The last boat's just gone, and every where's full.'

We were full too, as it was well into the season, but I felt sorry for them.

'I could put up a couple of beds in the lounge, and there is a sofa bed there. Would that do?'

'They said 'OK'; I'll send them up.'

The two young couples settled in, and I managed to chat in my basic French. I fed them and left them in the lounge.

Halfway through the night I thought I could smell burning; then I realised it was the pungent aroma of Galois cigarettes. We had a strictly non-smoking policy; it was a wooden bungalow and would have caught fire very quickly, and anyway we both hated the smell of cigarettes, particularly as it affected Ken's asthma.

We could not believe our eyes when we knocked and went in to the lounge. Empty drink bottles were scattered everywhere and they had been playing cards, smoking and drinking all night. I was surprised that no guests had complained, but assumed the French group had been reasonably quiet. We asked them to stop immediately but my French was not good enough to tell them what I thought of their behaviour. Maybe it was normal for them, but I was glad to see them go in the morning. It took me days to rid the room of the stale pub-like smell.

Our preference was for families, styling ourselves as a 'Family Guest House.' As well as the two cots and high chairs, we had acquired two pushchairs and a baby back pack.

For a while, until the repairs became too time consuming, we also had some bicycles for hire.

There were at first a few problems with having young children. Mothers with babies did not realise that our borehole water supply could not cope with daily nappy washing. Then we included disposable nappies in our 'shop,' and life was easier for the parents and for us.

One incident occurred which could have had serious repercussions. As a female guest walked out of the lounge one evening, the large, heavy telephone bell which had been on the wall above the door, fell on her head. Fortunately she had a sense of humour and was not hurt.

We made sure the bell was moved to a safer position after that.

We often needed a sense of humour ourselves when dealing with some of our guests. On one occasion a guest failed to turn up for dinner. He had arrived the previous day with his wife and young child. She was very agitated, and said that her husband had gone to one of the Pubs for a pre-dinner drink.

He still had not returned by bedtime, and we had visions of his being lost or falling down a bank.

There was no street lighting at all on Sark, so we always left a torch in each room for guests' use, but theirs was still by the bedside.

We were just about to ring Hap, who was doing his stint as voluntary Constable, when the phone rang. 'You got a guest missing, eh?' He sounded amused. 'Well he's looking at the gaol; from the inside.' The Sark Gaol, built in 1856, was a tourist attraction, being one of the smallest in the world.

'My bloody nephew got him drunk. You want this guest back, eh?' The last thing we wanted was a drunk guest. 'Can't you get him to take a swipe at you, then you have an excuse to lock him up for the night,' I asked.

Ken went down to the gaol, but try as they might, the guest could not be egged on to hit out at Hap. My heart sank as I could hear strains of, 'She'll be coming round the mountain when she comes,' echoing up the driveway.

As his wife said he became violent when drunk, she had barricaded herself in their room. We plied him with as much coffee as he could take, and tucked him down in a vacant room.

As we wearily went to bed, I began to realise that our responsibilities did not end with just giving bed and board.

14

Some of the situations were not at all amusing. On one occasion an elderly guest had a stroke. It would have been less complicated if he had not been on the top bunk of one of the 'family rooms.'

We had decided early on in our venture, price reductions would be on the number sharing a room, rather than ages of children. For the first year we found it was not economical to have two reduced charge children occupying a whole room by themselves. So we offered larger families who wanted to share a room, up to two thirds reduction in some cases. Occasionally, as in this instance, four adults decided to share, though we did not recommend it.

There was a tentative knock on our bedroom door at two in the morning (why did these things always happen in the dead of night?)

'So sorry to bother you, but Dad doesn't seem too well.'

'Too much rich Sark cream!' I thought, but went in to have a look, while Ken grumbled sleepily and turned over in bed.

The snoring breathing, dribbling mouth and lack of responses from the elderly man, galvanised me into action. Despite the fact that he was on the top bunk, I managed to turn him on his side to stop him choking, asking his relatives to call Ken to ring urgently for the Doctor.

In those days the telephone exchange was manned in a tiny cottage on Sark for twenty four hours a day by Mrs West or her relief, Mrs Grant. Whichever was on duty at night slept on a camp bed. The receivers were operated by cranking a handle, which activated the exchange board with a bell and flashing light. It was a social hub, and while not a centre of gossip, the wonderful operators knew all that went on round the Island. I seldom knew anyone's number, just asked for the person. The operators would say something like, 'oh yes, well she's gone to her sister's, I'll put you through.'

Once I was trying to contact a friend, but there was no answer. Having just stoked the Rayburn to have a bath, and not wanting to waste the hot water, I said to Mrs West, 'Well never mind, I'm just going to have a bath. I'll ring later.' While I was enjoying my soak, the phone rang but I left it.

Apparently it had been my friend. Next day when I rang her she immediately asked with a laugh, 'did you have a nice bath?' Mrs West must have commented on my planned ablutions.

On this occasion Ken only had to crank the handle twice and told Mrs West the problem. Immediately she phoned the Doctor, and after he visited and confirmed my suspicions, she put the emergency service into action. Within a quarter of an hour the Sark ambulance arrived at Camp Farm and the St John rescue launch started on its half hour journey from Guernsey. Victor and his driver were strong men. With the help of the patient's son and

Ken, the whole bunk bed was lifted down and through the bedroom door. The Sark ambulance arrived at the Maseline harbour with the patient and his family, just as the launch from Guernsey rounded the headland. It was a well practiced and perfected system, which had the patient in Hospital in Guernsey within an hour after the Doctor's visit.

I was pleased to hear that our guest made a good recovery and they all came back the following year. I insisted on separate rooms, however.

This family was numbered among the many friends we made over the years. Some came back year after year; calling 'Camp Farm' their 'Island retreat.' Some had their favourite rooms.

One daughter came back on her honeymoon with her new husband. Although that was not without its crisis

'Chris, I've lost my engagement ring,' she wailed one morning. We turned her room, the lounge and the dining room upside down.

'When did you last have it?'

'I washed my husband's socks, and that's when I last saw it. Could it have gone down the drain do you think?' I had dreadful thoughts of looking in the septic tank, but then I had another idea. We went to the line where the socks hung dripping, fortunately hung by the top. Sure enough, there it glittered, nestled in the toe. 'Next time, I suggest you take it off ... and put it somewhere safe!'

The happy times far outweighed the anxious moments, but our changed lifestyle had its own restrictions. I found it difficult always to be 'on duty' twenty four hours a day for seven days a week.

On a good season this could be for twenty eight weeks of the year. I was always supposed to be sweetness and light, whatever the time or request. I know I was not always gracious, particularly if the monstrosity was misbehaving or I was in the middle of a baking session. Sometimes I would be found by a guest, as I was sitting in a deckchair in the middle of the day, usually with a bowl of half peeled potatoes or peas to shell.

Any comments of, 'nice for some people,' got rather short shrift. Many a time I was tempted to retort, 'I bet your day doesn't start at five thirty in the morning and end at midnight!'

With envy I watched people trekking off for the day and wistfully remembered our carefree holidays on Sark. Somehow we seldom had time to go to the beach now, but having our dog Hugo gave me a good excuse to walk onto the near headland after the washing up to give him some exercise and me a breath of fresh air.

It was then, when I looked over cliffs ablaze with gorse, and smelled the pungently sweet mix of horse manure and honeysuckle; I knew it was all worth it.

15

For the first few years, conscious that we had a heavy loan to repay we decided to stay open all year. Many other places closed, as Sark in winter was wet and windy, with little for visitors to do. Sometimes there were workmen from Guernsey, but they preferred to stay near a pub. Occasionally hardy walkers came for a few days, but mostly our guests were temporary replacements for the two bank managers or relief Methodist or Anglican ministers.

When our resident Anglican minister had to be away for a few weeks, we were delighted to look after his replacement. Rev. Timothy was a frail looking, saintly man well on in years. He was always impeccably dressed, quiet and sober in habit, and was prone to take daily long walks, using his umbrella as a walking stick. I assumed he never put it up in the strong winds, which we were seldom without. If he did, I had visions of his sailing away like an ecclesiastical 'Mary Poppins.'

Mrs Hill, although about the same age as the Reverend, was quite a different story. One day in late

October, at the end of our first year I had a call from Dr King.

'Look, I've got an elderly lady in Little Sark,' he sounded unusually hesitant, 'she has had a stroke but pointedly refuses to go to Guernsey.' He continued, 'it has been twenty four hours and she is no worse, so I was wondering if you would like to look after her for a while?' There was a pause, 'trouble is, the son who is looking after her hasn't a clue.' He paused again.

'I hear you are opening for the winter. She is not the easiest of customers, but could you take her in for a while?'

I had heard about Mrs Hill and her strong personality, but we badly needed the money, and apparently she was 'not short of a bob or two' as my Dad would say. I agreed, and that afternoon my patient arrived. As did her dog. I was not happy about the yappy Jack Russell, but it was too late to change my mind.

Fortunately our dog Hugo was easy going, and put up with the canine visitor. In the end they became good friends and Hugo taught the smaller dog some manners.

I had nursed many patients after a stroke, so this was no problem. After a cup of tea and some homemade cake I started as I meant to continue. Too much softness was no help in the healing process.

'Right, Mrs Hill,' I said firmly as soon as she was finished, 'time to get up for a sit in the chair.' My patient mumbled something. 'Sorry didn't catch that. Try just one word.' I certainly heard the resounding 'No' that time.

'Look, I could just let you lie there all day, getting bedsores and deteriorating to a zombie, or we can work together on this.' I wondered if I had gone too far.

Too late to go back, so I tried a different tack. 'I hear you have had an interesting life, and I would love to hear all about it.' I saw a glint of humour in her bright blue eyes, and I knew the healing process had begun.

Daily my patient made progress. Even the dog and I had an armed truce when he learned who fed him. After four weeks, Mrs Hill left Camp Farm with only a slight limp. I had found the combination of nursing and cooking breakfast, lunch, supper, and supplying innumerable snacks and cups of tea, exhausting. There were times to sit and chat, however. It was good therapy and the tales Mrs Hill told of world travel and of her time as a cook in a Canadian Lumber Camp, exciting. I particularly delighted in one of her favourite sayings, when we had been chatting for a long time. 'My dear Chris, we really have been hung up by the tongue today!'

By the time Mrs Hill left, my thoughts of possibly opening an old people's home were banished forever, but I did agree to take another patient the following winter.

Mrs Bentley had also had a stroke but was more ambulant and just wanted a few weeks of care and 'cosseting' as the Doctor put it. It did not mean so much work, and the nursing was minimal. She was a true lady and was obviously used to servants, but did not treat me as one. Always immaculately dressed this slim, white haired guest was appreciative of all I did for her. Which of course made me want to do more.

I was still able to continue helping Ken with outside repair work. All of the fifty two small windows in the conservatory had lost their putty, and I thought I would like to try my hand at its replacement. I had read that if *Pollifiller* was mixed with half water and half gloss paint it worked like putty. I thought I would try it and donned my grubbiest clothes and mixed a large dish-full.

It was a rare, sunny, wind-free day; the birds had started to sing and I thought I could smell the grass growing. I looked over at the front lawn, thinking it would soon need cutting. To my horror, I saw 'La Dame's' electric invalid chair stop by our gate.

She got out and started to walk across the lawn using her stick to support her arthritic hip. I rushed over, putty and pallet knife in hand.

'It's alright, Mrs Davies. I haven't come to see you. I can see you are busy.' I could see a twitch of humour on her lips. 'I have come to see my friend Beatrice. Maybe we could have a cup of tea and a slice of your famous cake, when you have finished.' I abandoned the rock hard batch of putty, and changed to cleaner clothes. After all, it was not every day that your 'Head of State' came to tea.

Creux Harbour

Camp farm front and back

View from front lawn and dining room

La Coupee and Grand Greve beach

Transport Sark-style

Ken with Goats

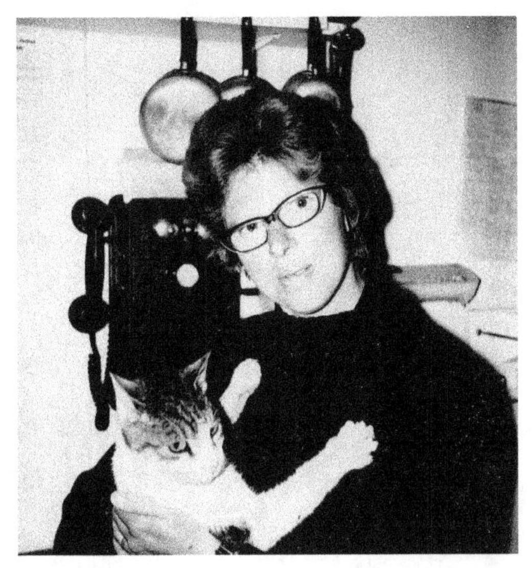

Chris with Kelly Pedro and Mischief

16

The early tensions between Ken and me were settling and we began to realise what this new life involved. Living and working together twenty-four hours a day was a far cry from the usual marriage. In London, we saw each other briefly in the morning as we rushed off to work. In the evening, I was often working, or Ken would be out with the badminton youth club or the scouts group he ran.

I discovered that the fairy tales had it all wrong. It was impossible to live together happily ever after. Or maybe Prince Charming did not scatter coal all over the kitchen floor when he stoked the Rayburn, or pull all the bedclothes off when he got up to the toilet in the freezing night. I bet the princess never had monthly problems or days when nothing went right. I was quite sure not many couples had to sleep in a storeroom when all the bedrooms were occupied, where a sudden movement sent a shower of toilet rolls or packets of cornflakes cascading over their heads. Nor were they woken in the night by the rattling water pump filling the tank, when a guest made a nocturnal visit to the bathroom. But we survived and learned to laugh a little together.

One of our concerns was trying to resolve the problem of requests from friends and relatives who wanted to visit us. Naturally they wished to see this Utopia we had raved about. The question was 'to pay or not to pay?' We could not afford always to offer a room *gratis* but it seemed so mercenary to charge. Usually, we compromised and offered reduced rates in off peak times. This suited most people as we also had a little more time to show them our favourite beaches and walks. There were a few, mostly distant relatives and friends who seldom contacted us, who did not understand that this was our livelihood. They obviously resented having to pay anything at all and I grumpily felt like saying, 'OK; how would you like to give us a percentage of your earnings!'

One spring, both Ken's parents and mine decided to visit us at the same time. None of them had been to Sark before and I wondered how they would cope with the restrictions of Island life. No big shops to wander round; no tarseal roads or street lighting, and no car or public transport. They would have to walk everywhere, but there was a lovely garden to sit in and they were coming to see us in any case. It would be a rest for Ken's father, Bert, who was a self-employed builder and decorator and not at all well. I was very fond of this slight, wiry man and sad that he and Ken were not very close.

Bert had wanted Ken to join him in his business, and knew his son had a natural aptitude. However Ken's mother wanted him to be a 'white collar worker'. Ken would have been happier following in his father's footsteps.

Elsie, Ken's mother was a staunch Methodist and teetotaller. I knew she was a little disappointed in me as a daughter-in-law. When Ken and I were first married and settled in London, she was delighted that her asthmatic son had a nurse to look after him. At nearly thirty, he had still been living at home and his mother had thought him a settled bachelor. Then, what a shock when Ken gave up his prestigious job in advertising and moved to this odd little island. I think she thought it was all my doing. In fact, Ken knew his days were numbered in advertising; it was only a matter of time before younger men stepped into his shoes. It was a *cut and thrust* type of business.

My parents: beautiful stepmother Phyl (more like a sister, and I loved her like one) and my father Wilf, had lived in the country much of their married life, so I hoped Sark would not be too much of a culture shock. Diagnosed with Parkinson's disease some years previously, Pop was well controlled on medication.

I was delighted that he had wanted to see our new life and home. I knew he hated travelling, and had a pathological fear of any means of transport other than by car, so I knew what a special effort he was making.

With just a week to go, I had a phone call from my mother. 'I'm so sorry, Chrissie; Pop is not very well. He has had one of his bad headaches,' she sighed. 'We just can't make it.' I could hear she was near tears. I felt terribly let down. Having spent days in preparation and in cleaning, I did not feel very sympathetic.

'Well come without him!'

'You know I can't do that.' She retreated into anger, more for her husband than me. 'Well maybe some other time.' Which we both sadly knew was not likely.

Ken's parents duly arrived and I could see that this rural life amazed them. They had both lived in London all their lives, seldom moving from the areas of their birth. Sometimes I could hardly believe Ken was their son, as he was far more adventurous.

After they settled in, we all sat in the warm kitchen for a cup of tea. Suddenly Bert hooted with laughter.

'Well, I don't know, I feel sorry for your poor guests! Do you have to dose them with bicarb every day?'

'What on earth ... ?' I followed the direction of his riveted gaze. Try as I might, I could not convince him that the large store of bicarbonate of soda was to clean the

Melamine crockery. We all laughed, but I could see poor Elsie, who had little sense of the ridiculous, saw little humour.

The week went quickly, and fortunately the spring weather stayed fine. We took some walks but the climb up and down to the beaches was too much for Bert, who became breathless easily. Dear Dad, this was the only time he ever visited us. Soon after he was diagnosed with Cancer. When Ken's presence was needed in London, of course he had to go, even though it was the height of the season.

By that time, we had made friends with another couple, Peter and Marjorie who had just moved to Sark with their three children, to run an established guest house and tea garden. They were very helpful while Ken was away, and we all became great friends from that time.

17

My first planting of vegetables before Ken returned to
Sark at Easter, proved to be a success, although it was
uncertain at first what was in which row, thanks to
Hugo's pulling up all the pegs. The ground was very
fertile and Ken soon mastered vegetable growing on a
grand scale, with enough potatoes, carrots, leeks and
cabbages for guests and for sale.

The first year, we decided to ask Hap to plough the
back field and help us to put in a good crop of potatoes in
early spring. He had a special machine with a hopper and
seats either side. The loose potatoes were tipped into the
hopper and Ken and I sat precariously on either side, on
the uncomfortable metal seats which had holes
underneath. The freezing wind blew up through the holes
until Hap took pity and gave us old sacks to give a little
padding. We had to push potatoes as fast as we could
down shoots between our knees and then blades behind
furrowed, to bury them in the soil. It was freezing and
tiring work not helped by Hap's jocular comments like;

'be sure you put them up the right way, eh?' I really did think there was a right way up till I saw his wide grin.

With excitement we watched the dark green shoots unfurl, grow tall and eventually start to flower.

We tried various types of potatoes, as we were not sure which would do best. The 'first earlies' we were able to dig at the beginning of June. Only those who have been imprisoned in a city can understand the joy that a country spring can give. My heart soared with the skylarks as we went in to the field to dig the first new potatoes.

It was a sensual pleasure to ease a fork deep into the rich dark soil and turn it over, pulling gently at the stem. The gleaming, creamy potatoes tumbled out, some still attached to the root. Another dig and usually the biggest potatoes that had nestled in the soil popped into sight. I never tired of seeing the first new potatoes. Later in the year, with the second 'earlies' and the 'main-crop', we asked Hap's help again, this time with his potato harvester. This was a rattling huge machine that dug out potatoes, stones, weeds and clods of earth and threw them on to a conveyer belt. Perched on the top, Ken and I and a couple of other helpers, had to grab the good potatoes off the belt into bags, before they all disappeared back down a shute onto the ground. 'Got to get them all,' said Hap, for once quite serious.

'Any that go back into the soil will grow again next year. You don't want that. You need good seed potatoes each year, eh?'

He would not accept payment for his help and the use of equipment. 'How about you come and help Sam and me with our planting and harvesting, eh?' We were happy to; it was a good arrangement.

The first year was a great success. We grew enough potatoes to supply ourselves for the year, feed all our guests and sell the surplus. The second year was a disaster. As soon as the little dark green shoots started to show, we had heavy mists. This was quite common in May, with the sea still cold but the air warming.

Sometimes the fog was all around, with the eerie sound of the foghorn drifting across the fields. Often it cleared quickly from the top of the Island, yet the sea was still invisible. At times like that, I felt alone in a strange world, floating somewhere between Heaven and Earth, with the sound of the waves breaking far below on the rugged rocks.

After a week of this weather, one morning I went to the back of the house, and looked at the field. It was black. All the lovely little shoots had withered.

I phoned Hap. 'It's the same for us,' he muttered, 'the bloody blight! Good job we left the main crop till later.' So we planted the rest of the field when the weather improved. We were fated to have few potatoes that year, as they also failed to thrive. This time it was eelworm. Fatal to the crop, it was like the 'foot and mouth' of the vegetable world. The whole field had to be sterilised and we could not grow potatoes there for seven years. We were lucky that this was not a main source of income for us.

The following year, Hap ploughed another patch and we started again. 'Of course, don't forget to treat for wireworm, eh?' He had the pleasure to inform us. 'What on earth's that?' Was there no end to the things we had to learn?

'New grassland has to be treated before you can grow potatoes. The Morris' have already had potatoes in that back field. S'why you got eelworm. Land must have been affected. You were lucky with the first year, eh?'

Even with potatoes in the side field and vegetables at the back, there was still a good acre of lawn and rough grass, and a long grassy driveway to mow. We had to do better than the temperamental lawn mower we bought from the Morris'.

From people leaving the Island we bought a newer roller mower and an ancient 'Merritiller Cultivator,' to help with the weeding of vegetables. An 'Allen Scythe' completed our mechanical help. It was worth its weight in gold. Almost as old as the first mower, this was robust, with scissor-like shears at the front. Ken was able to cut long grass, and later, even a small field of hay. At last we felt we were making our dream of a smallholding a reality. 'What we now need,' decided Ken, 'is some livestock.' In that decision, we did not realise we had set ourselves on a whole new adventure.

18

One of the main disadvantages of Island life was the freight cost added to all bought items. Trying to keep our Guest House rates low, meant we had to cut costs to the minimum. Having a few hens and our own eggs for the Guest House was one way to do that. 'It won't be too much extra work,' said I, in all innocence, 'I'll look after them.'

The Morris' had once kept chickens, so we called to ask their advice. 'A good idea, my dears. You can have our old hen house on wheels for a few pounds,' was Mrs Morris' response. She gave us the address of a breeder of chickens on the mainland and we bought a book on keeping poultry.

'Look at this,' Ken was enthusiastic as he showed me pictures of a 'fold unit'. 'You make an inverted 'V' run and cover it with wire on two sides and one end. The bottom is open so the hens can scratch around in the grass without escaping and the other end butts onto the hen house.'

'Won't the ground get sour?' I remembered my parents having a few hens and how the ground soon became dry and dusty in summer and boggy in winter.

'No, of course not. The idea is to move run and hens every few days.' He seemed very sure of himself. 'The house has wheels so it should be easy enough.' However it proved to be more difficult than expected as it was a very heavy building. Ken eventually devised a lever system, using a length of four by four timber, which worked well until we bought our donkey, who pulled it around.

We were not sure what age pullets to order and made our first mistake by buying ten birds at seven weeks old. They were just out of the warmed, deep litter barns and unused to the cool spring weather. Although we padded the corners of the hen house with hay and left the perches in place, the young birds huddled and smothered those underneath. My impatience with these silly birds was born then, and I never lost it.

The second batch of twenty five, we chose to buy pullets of sixteen weeks old. 'Point of lay,' said our helpful book, 'is usually at twenty one weeks.' We watched the calendar like expectant parents. Sure enough, exactly at twenty one weeks we found our first shiny brown egg, glistening in a nest box.

'It's awfully small,' complained Ken.

'Of course, they are pullet eggs! They will be better when they get into the swing of it.' I was pleased to air my superior knowledge.

It was an achievement to use our own eggs for guests' meals and word spread rapidly around the Island. 'Chris, any chance of a few eggs?' Was a regular request.

Realising there was a side line here, we decided to buy more hens in the autumn. They were a hybrid cross of 'Rhode Island Red' and 'Light Suffolk'. The advantage was a heavy bird that laid well but did not have high food consumption. The disadvantage was that their laying life, while prolific, lasted only for about two years. 'Birds normally moult in late autumn,' said our book. 'They will then cease to lay until the spring.' That was a concern, as I soon had many customers wanting eggs throughout the whole year, not just at peak laying time.

We found that our birds kept laying in spring, summer and their first winter, moulting only on their second autumn. By buying new hens in spring and autumn, I was able to keep my customers satisfied.

Eventually my few hens had blossomed to two hundred birds. We now had a chicken farm. We even discovered that some of the plumper birds made good boiling fowls. A bonus income. I never quite developed the knack of pulling the neck sharply to kill instantly, so was quite happy to leave that and the preparation of plucking and drawing, to Ken.

My handy husband made three other fold unit runs for smaller houses which we bought locally. Each unit had its own water dispenser and feeder and run. At first I made a hot mash for the hens, using potato peelings. The smell was pungent and reminiscent of a brewery. I hated the smell and abandoned it eventually, as I felt it did nothing for my reputation as a good cook. We soon invested in self-help feeders, adding grit and oyster shell to the feed. Our book informed us this was necessary for the hen's digestion and to make strong shells. Added to this was a daily scattering of wheat and some cabbage stalks. I began to wonder if it would not have been easier and cheaper to buy the blessed eggs, but the taste of a new laid egg surpassed all other and was much appreciated by our guests. Sometimes it was so new laid that I was standing over the hens waiting for enough to finish my breakfast preparation.

It was not long before I had orders from all over the Island. Blithely I had thought it a useful extra income. We had no trouble selling all we produced, but if we had charged the price per dozen to compensate for the feed, grain and the time spent washing and grading, no one would have been interested.

Once or twice I put some to preserve in Isinglass. They were hardly nestled in the sticky mess in the large crock pots than the phone would ring.

'Chris, we are desperate, the chef forgot to order enough eggs, *please* do you have any spare?' So out they came again.

<h1 style="text-align:center">19</h1>

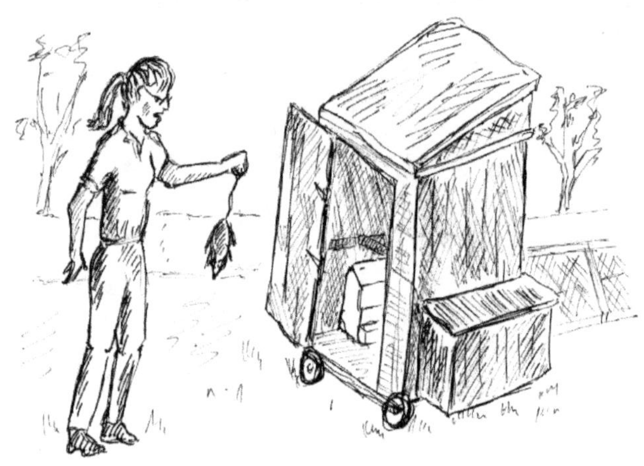

A disadvantage of the self-help feeders was their attraction to rats. Once I was refilling one in the large house and heard a scuffle. I pulled the feeder forward, and there was the mother of all rats, sitting fat and pregnant cleaning her whiskers. The long tail was spread towards me, and without really thinking I bent and grabbed it. I swung the rat round and smashed its head onto the wall with a sickening crack. It was only afterwards that I remembered stories of rats climbing up their own tails to bite the hand that held them. The feel of the skin stripping slowly away from the bone like a banana skin, stayed with me for years.

Another of our animal problems was the proliferation of rabbits. Hugo did his best. This unfortunately resulted in flattened vegetables, a muddy dog and a worse mess than if he had left well alone. So we decided a cat would be the answer. A tiny, black spitting bundle of pin-like claws, Inky never became other than the semi-wild cat he was born. Jim, our carter, gave the kitten to us with a comment of, 'here, you'll need one of these; train it to catch rabbits; the mother was a good 'un.'

As soon as he was old enough Ken said it was time for Inky to go to work, and introduced him to a rabbit hole. Down he shot and came up a moment later with a young rabbit in his mouth.

After that day all he required was a daily dish of warm goat's milk, as he fed himself. He did more than that. He redeemed several Pounds in rabbit tail bounty during his lifetime. The local Constable's office offered a 'bob a knob' for tails taken to their office, as rabbits were such a pest. Inky soon learned to bring the back legs to the kitchen door, to exchange fluffy tail for warm milk. He was an intelligent animal but was not always able to avoid traps and snares set for his quarry.

Once he returned with a broken leg, which had been caught in a trap. They were illegal, but some farmers still used them; we guessed he had been discovered and let free and I hoped the farmer had a good scratching from the enraged cat. Another time, Inky came back with a wire snare round his neck. He had chewed through it and his tongue was lacerated. In both cases, treatment was as traumatic for us as for him. We all needed first aid.

Kelly was quite a different cat.

One, day Paul our local retired vet rang. 'Look, I hope you don't mind my ringing but I wonder if you'd like another cat?'

'Well, no not really ... '

'I just can't do it!' He sounded upset, 'you know that old Dr Cooper died and his wife is leaving the Island? Well she is going into a flat in London and can't take a cat. She wants me to put it down.'

'Is it a hunter?'

'Well, actually ... ,' his hesitancy should have warned me. 'Let me just bring him round and you can decide.' He rang off before I could reply.

It was love at first sight for me. A pure bred, aristocratic Manx cat, Kelly had been the spoiled pet of

Dr Cooper. He had a neat tabby cap and waistcoat; the rest was pure white, but the strangest part was his very long back legs and the absence of a tail. I could not resist the face-splitting meow he gave as Paul opened his cat carrier. When it was known we had taken on Kelly, advice was freely offered.

'He's a very fussy eater; and watch out for your furniture; he'll have it in shreds. He was spoiled rotten.'

They had not reckoned on Hugo. Refusing to eat what was put down, Kelly starved for a few days, watching with disdain as our permanently hungry dog wolfed his rations. The third day, he dotted Hugo soundly on his nose and swallowed his pride with his breakfast. The furniture was not a problem as he discovered the great outdoors and became an efficient mouser. Unfortunately, he delighted in bringing his catch to eat by the dining room windows, usually at supper time when the guests were enjoying their dinner.

We also dubbed him 'The Foreman.' No new box of supplies went unexplored and a ladder propped against a wall was an open invitation. The sight of Kelly, balancing without a tail, had me in fits of silent laughter, but I would never hurt his dignity.

20

Our plan of being self-supporting pointed towards one day having bees. As far as I was concerned that day could not be far enough away. It was the only part of our enterprise I could not face. I had been stung once as a child and the reaction was painful and long lasting. It left me with a fear that bees were able to sense and made them aggressive in my presence.

There were several beekeepers on the Island and one, Mr Smith, became a patient of mine for a while. My duties were not arduous, but it was clear that he would soon have to leave Sark. During our chats I became fascinated by the stories he told me about the life of bees.

'Did you know,' he would say, 'that when a worker has found a good source of pollen and nectar, she will show the others where it is?' He smiled at me. 'Clever little things! She will do a dance on the alighting board of the hive to show them the location.'

'You said 'she', are they all female?'

'The workers, yes. The drones are the male; only use is to breed with the Queen on her maiden flight. Then a lot of them are bumped off!' He wheezed in laughter. 'Should happen to all us useless males.'

'No, don't say that. I shall miss you. You've made me see how amazing bees are. I've always been a bit scared of them. Ken wants to have a few hives, and I can see why.'

'Look I've had an idea; how would you and your hubby like to take a couple of my hives?'

'I couldn't do that: I am sure you could sell them.'

'What say you take them as exchange, instead of giving me a bill? That should keep you both happy. 'Nuff said; decision made.' He would not change his mind and that was how we started in the beekeeping business.

Before my patient left, he gave us instructions on moving the hives. Fortunately it was winter and the bees were semi-dormant, not liking the cold. We had a word with Sam, who had been a beekeeper himself.

'Best to move them at dusk. I'll bring my link box at the back of the tractor. You can both stand on it and steady the hives.' I was not so sure about that, but agreed.

The men blocked the entrance to the hives and gently lifted them on to the bucket shaped link box.

'Careful not to jog them,' was Sam's instruction. 'Don't want to wake the little darlings.'

While Ken stood on the back, I was happy to be on the footplate well away. However, relieved at arriving, I was a little too keen to get off the tractor and caught my foot on the bucket's release lever. With a resounding thump everything landed hard on the ground. Our quick scatter in three different directions would have done credit to the best slapstick comedies. It gave Hap fuel for weeks as he had been watching at a safe distance. Our dislike of bees was one thing we had in common. Later I sometimes had my own laugh when he worked in his fields next door, near the hives. The bees seemed to know that the only thing he liked about them was their honey.

That was our next problem. How to obtain and extract honey. We bought a book and read it. We read it again, and it still sounded like a foreign language.

'A hive consists of a floor and platform, on which is placed the brood box. A queen excluder follows and then the supers. In these are frames which contain the foundation, or you can have sections for comb honey. The number of supers depends on the honey flow. On top of the supers you place the quilt and the roof,' and so on.

The solution, we found in an old out-of-print book from a junk shop. It started by assuming the reader did not know what a bee looked like. Which was almost our case. It was so good that I soon became an informed, theoretical beekeeper and could even hold a reasonable conversation with Ken on the subject.

My calm husband had just the right temperament for beekeeping and made an excellent job of it. Sark proved the right place too, as the honey flow was longer than elsewhere, providing certain care was taken. As bees make honey to eat during the non-productive cold months, taking it without replacement would starve them. Beekeepers generally make a sugar-water to feed during winter. On Sark, a late-flowering tree ivy gave a good honey for the bees, but it was bitter to our palate, so it was left in the hive for the bees' winter food.

Through Sam we bought a second-hand honey extractor. This looked like a hand operated spin dryer, and worked rather like one. The full frames of honey, after the cappings were cut off with a hot knife, were placed four at a time on the internal racks. A handle at the top enabled Ken to spin the honey from the wax honeycomb, and a tap at the bottom released the bubbling golden stream into jars.

Our smallholding was growing.

21

I had heard it said that only eccentrics kept goats, and by the time we had ours, I was inclined to agree. In my mind, we had to be mad to be leading this type of life, so what was one more proof?

For some time, we had known about the wild goats on the cliffs. They were really escapees from the farm of an old lady who lived not far from Camp Farm. We had heard that she now lived on her own after the death of her elder sister. She was related to a famous painter and both sisters were reputably very talented artists in their own right. We had also heard she would never sell a painting, but that was not what we wanted. We were only interested in the goats. Thinking it was polite to ask permission from Miss Tupper, one sparkling morning found us walking up the seemingly endless drive, trying to avoid the encroaching brambles. As the path widened, the barn like house was revealed. Shimmering in the golden light the wooden building looked deserted.

We knocked several times at the open door. Dogs, cats and chickens wandered in and out, accompanied by the busiest cloud of flies I had ever seen. 'Come on, there's no-one at home.' Ken was all for leaving. I had not been a district nurse for nothing.

'She must be here. They said she never goes out. Anybody there?' I shouted.

We nearly jumped out of our skins, as a voice just the other side of the door bellowed, 'Come in, come in!'

The old lady sitting in the cluttered room in an old armchair looked a hundred, but the merry sparkle in her eyes made us realise that she was far from senile. Piles of clothes, crockery, and beautiful paintings framed and unframed were jumbled everywhere.

'I'm a bit deaf,' bellowed Miss Tupper. 'If you've come for a painting, I don't have any spare ones. Have a cup of tea, now you are here.' By this time the flies had discovered my tender skin and I was hopping from one foot to the other, trying to avoid their sharp nip. Even Ken was looking a little uncomfortable.

Over a cup of very strong tea we managed at last to explain our errand. 'You're welcome to try,' the old lady said with a knowing chuckle. As soon as possible, we beat a hasty retreat, leaving the flies to their own devices; much fortified I was sure, by pints of our blood.

Helped by Hap's nephew Liam, we decided to tackle the goats on the cliffs a few days afterwards. Following his uncle's lead, Liam had developed a liking for my cake and a cup of tea, and often popped in for a chat.

We had become good friends so he was glad to assist us, but I was a little disconcerted to see his double barrelled shotgun tucked under his arm when he arrived.

To my, 'what on earth is that for? We want them alive.' He just winked and said, 'rabbits.' As soon as we were out on the cliffs, he innocently asked me if I would like to have a pot at a rabbit. Always keen to try something new, I followed his instructions. 'You just nestle the stock into your shoulder and point it at a rabbit then you pull the trigger.' There was a tremendous bang; I flew backwards and sat heavily on the bracken, sporting a very sore shoulder. 'Er, you should just pull one trigger at a time.' Liam said with a grin.

'You should have said; she could have broken her shoulder!' Ken was annoyed. He and Liam were not the best of friends. I think he disliked the time Hap's nephew spent in the kitchen chatting with me, but I enjoyed his teasing and jokes.

Some time passed before we saw our first group of goats, but try as we might, they were always one step ahead. Wearily we eventually had to admit defeat, understanding at last Miss Tupper's chuckle. The rabbit stew was tasty though, and we shared it with Liam.

We did no more for a while, then two mature goats literally dropped into our laps. We were over in Guernsey on a shopping trip and called to see an elderley lady who kept donkeys, as we had decided we would like a donkey too, so followed any lead.

However, she had none for sale. We were just about to leave to catch the boat home, when she said, 'you wouldn't like two goats would you? They are 'Golden Guernsey' breed; quite rare. Five pounds each.' She took us to a shed in the garden. They were the saddest animals I had ever seen. Their ginger-coloured coats were matted and in terrible condition and their hooves turned upwards like jester's shoes. They each had curving horns but had the sweetest deer-like faces. Caution was not one of my stronger points. 'We'll have them,' I said before Ken could open his mouth. When he did, it was with his usual common sense.

'And how are we to get them to the boat in half an hour?' He asked the lady.

'Don't worry. I have transport. I'll take you,'

There was just room for me with the two goats in the back of the old Ford Prefect, provided I poked their heads out of the side windows and held tight to their frayed collars. Just as we were approaching the harbour I looked through the back window. A man in a passing car was staring popeyed as if he could not believe his eyes.

Inevitably it was a wild and windy day and Ken had to carry each goat onto the boat over the heaving gangplank. We spent a wet and smelly rough return to Sark on the lower deck, hanging on to our frightened new purchases.

At least we now had our goats.

22

$\mathbf{S}$am came to our rescue again. 'These girls are full of red worm; you've got to drench them.' I had visions of dunking each goat in the bath. 'You have to give them a dose of medicine in a plastic bottle,' he patiently explained to us.

A large empty shampoo bottle was filled with the green sticky liquid. While I held the goat's head back, massaging the throat, Ken cocked his leg astride like a horse rider and inserted the bottle in her mouth. Most of the liquid ended up his sleeve at first, but he soon mastered the technique.

We never had this problem when we later had to drench with draft beer. It was the fisherman Bruce, who had also kept goats, who advised us when one of our goats ate heartily of laurel, a deadly poison. We thought she would die, as she was so very ill. Four hourly drenching all night and day restored her to an internally cleansed, hiccupping goat, and one addicted to beer for life.

Spring greens and a goat mix of crushed oats, bran and flaked maize soon restored the goats. With their hooves trimmed and golden coats gleaming, we were justly proud of our girls, named Lulu and Mimi by Ken.

One morning we discovered that Lulu's udder was filling. 'I thought they had to breed to give milk,' I said to Sam as he delivered our cow's milk one morning. (We had bought another book; this time on goat keeping). 'Well, not always. She's what you call a 'maiden milker.' I bet she'll do well if you do breed from her. Let's have a look.' He bent and squeezed the udder, and milk shot out of two holes in one teat. 'You've got a problem here. Look I'll show you how to milk.'

Gradually we learned one more lesson. I had many a boot- full or eye-full, till I learned to jet the streams to each edge of the bucket. Lulu was an impatient madam, and had to be watched. If the milker did not pay attention, she would wait until the bucket was nearly full, and then lift a leg and plonk it into the rich creamy milk. Sometimes we had to work one-handed, holding a leg aloft, or tying it back.

Mimi did not come into milk spontaneously, so we decided to take Sam's advice and breed from the two goats. 'Goats come into season from late summer through winter to late spring, their time occurring every three weeks and lasting one to three days,' said our Goat book. The trouble was, what to do about it?

Our carter Jim had a young billy, so we decided to borrow Willie; and regretted it every time the winds blew towards the house in the months of its stay.

We discovered then that it is the male goat that has the offensive smell; not the female. Soon all our work clothes were affected and the visits from our friends on the Island became noticeably less.

'A goat's gestation is about five months' said our book casually. As Willie had been with us for several months now, we could not be sure when, or even if, we would have additions to the family, but eventually it was certain that our ladies were in kid, and we tethered them nearer the house.

I was peeling the potatoes one afternoon when Mimi began to bleat loudly. Yelling for Ken, I dashed out to see the goat straining with her back legs splayed. A wet little nose resting on two tiny hooves popped out and the rest of the amber coloured kid slid to the ground. I broke the sack and cleared its mouth. Soon it rose shakily to its feet and staggered towards its mother. Mimi started to bleat again and out popped his brother. The afterbirth followed, and it was all over by the time Ken arrived. With the two kids suckling, Mimi went back to her interrupted grazing.

Lulu was a different story. A few days after Mimi, she also started to bleat; and bleat. It was, of course, just on dinner time, but fortunately the guests were happy to wait. Lulu was smaller than her sister and the birth was more difficult.

Eventually, after much straining and bleating, little Brandy Snap was born. A dark ginger, this little nanny was like a small faun, and I loved her from the first. We only had time to wrap her in a towel, as she was quite weak, when Lulu started bleating again. This time she was very distressed, and I could see it was a breach presentation. With memories of my Midwifery book, I managed to deliver the large buck at last, but it was dead. Leaving Ken to clear up, I changed and served a belated meal to our patient guests.

That was not the end of Lulu's problems. The afterbirth did not come away as it should. I eventually had to perform a manual evacuation, which could be fatal to humans, but the hardy goat survived. Fortunately, our guests had left the dining room by then.

We put Brandy to her mother, but Lulu was so engorged with milk for two, that the tiny scrap could not fix.

'We will have to feed her,' said Ken with concern, 'Or she won't last the night. Do you have a baby's bottle?' I had not planned for this, but came up with a brainwave.

'Look, we can make a hole in my surgical glove; it should feel like a teat.' We milked out the colostrum, which was vital for a new kid and filled the improvised 'bottle' for three-hourly feeds; spelling each other throughout the night. In the morning, we reduced the tension in Lulu's teats and Brandy was able to suckle; soon our newest addition began to grow and thrive.

23

It was not practicable to keep the two male kids. 'Good eating on those,' said a neighbouring farmer; 'fatten 'em up a bit first.' My idea of self sufficiency did not go that far. Reluctantly, we asked our retired vet Paul to put them to sleep. I had no qualms about eating our hens, but the thought of roasting a little goat made me feel sick. I vividly remembered visiting my brother, David, in his student days, when he and his friends invited me to a Greek banquet. The roast suckling goat kid was brought in with its little legs sticking in the air and an apple where its head had been.

We could not bear to part with Brandy, so she grew in beauty and in mischief. Running free for her first few months, she was the bane of the other animals. Scattering cats and chickens in all directions, she delighted in climbing up the chicken runs at full gallop. Once on the top ridge, she proceeded to herd the bewildered hens in and out of their houses, until we stopped her. It was beginning to put them off lay.

We could not be cross for long as she was such a clown. One, day I was in the kitchen washing up, with my back to the door.

Suddenly I heard an almighty banging and a muffled bleating. Brandy had not been able to resist a tin of dried crusts we kept on the floor by the Rayburn for special animal treats. Expecting to steal a quick mouthful before I noticed, she had not made allowance for her new small horns. Literally caught in the act, she proclaimed her indignation to the world, until I released her from the tin where her head was well and truly stuck.

Quick to make friends with Hugo, but also a constant tease, Brandy came for walks with us. She would pirouette in front of the poor dog on her dainty little hooves just out of reach. Pretending to butt him, she just stopped short each time. They both enjoyed a long ramble but Brandy did not care much for the beach; she hated to get her hooves wet. Hugo bettered her there as he loved to swim. When he clambered out of the sea, he enjoyed a good shake all over her, and us, if we did not move fast enough. It was amusing to hear the holiday makers, 'look, Mum at those two nice dogs; Oh! One has got *horns!*'

One of Brandy Snap's closest friends, and I suspect a father substitute, was our donkey Pedro. He arrived soon after we bought Lulu and Mimi and was one of our happier inspirations. For Brandy he was the one to run to, when the world was unkind. She could be seen running up his back, while he was lying down. When tired she curled up and snuggled into his thick grey hair. He never seemed to mind, even when she nibbled his long ears, but sometimes he would blow down his nostrils at her when she was too naughty.

All the extra milk was a great boon to the guest house. It was necessary to continue feeding the goats well, but the rich creamy milk was its own reward. We discovered that only when we inadvertently tethered them near strong flavoured vegetation, did the milk have a distinctly unpleasant flavour. I used it exclusively for the evening milky drinks and in cooking. The guests were also given a choice between goat's and cow's milk at breakfast, and often the children were the most adventurous. Some guests vowed they would 'never touch the stuff!' One man in particular had relished his nightly Horlicks. 'Glad you didn't give me any of that goat muck. I was in Malta for years and I grew to hate the stuff.' I decided not to disillusion him.

We had more milk that we could use, so Ken tried cheese making. One of our growing stock of instruction books, told him how. He produced a semi hard very palatable cheese and soon we had orders for that, too. He sometimes raided the larder to try new flavours, but I did draw the line at a bright red one coloured with cochineal.

24

If Paul had not decided to sell his two pony traps and harness, perhaps we would not have thought of getting a donkey. The idea had crossed our minds that a pony would be an added attraction for the many children who stayed with us. Having had some experience with bad tempered ponies, I had visions of irate parents and tearful children. The natural transition was to the universally lovable, cuddly, long-eared donkey. In reality, we found them crafty, stubborn, unpredictable, infuriating animals. Also utterly captivating, as individual as people and far more intelligent than many.

We bought Paul's equipment first just in case we decided to enlarge our menagerie one day. After a few weeks of looking longingly at it, we decided to investigate our local area for a suitable donkey. The trip to Guernsey, when we bought Mimi and Lulu, had left us disappointed but still resolute. It is a fact that the more unattainable a thing is, the more desirable it seems. By this time, we had decided we just could not live without a donkey. It would be useful to cart our produce and take me shopping, and the visitors would love it.

'Look at this,' Ken pointed to an advertisement in a paper he was reading. 'For sale, grey donkey at just 45 pounds; to good home; large, eleven hands. Good with children; suitable to pull cart.' It certainly seemed ideal. A bit too good, I thought, but we convinced ourselves that all would be well.

It took many phone calls and complicated and expensive arrangements to transport our purchase from the mainland, but at last he was on his way. Ken went down to the harbour to meet 'Pedro' as we had decided to call him. We should have been warned when the owner was casual about a name or many details, but by that time our minds were set. Sam came to our aid once more and delivered our new purchase in a horse box.

'Hope you know what you have let yourself into,' was his less than encouraging comment. 'He isn't very well, and that looks like mange to me. I had better disinfect the horse-box.'

Sure enough, when we asked our friend Paul, the vet, to pop round and give Pedro the once over he confirmed it. 'Mange is hard to cure and very infectious. Keep him away from the other animals. I'll send some lotion round.' He looked increasingly distressed.

'This animal has been badly treated; see how he flinches when you approach his head; and listen to that cough. I bet he has had strangles.'

'What on earth's that?' We were becoming more and more concerned. We had been sold a sad animal, but were now even more determined to do the best for him, 'and what can we do to help?'

'It's a bit like croup; it responds well to a good cough mixture,' he laughed, 'don't know how you'll give him that!' Ingenious Ken eventually worked out a way of giving Pedro a sandwich, spread thickly with sticky cough mixture. It went down very well.

As Paul led the reluctant donkey around the back lawn, we noticed a strange kick in one back leg. It was almost as if he was kicking himself in the buttock. 'I see he has a 'string halt' as well; it is a sort of spasm in his tendon. You know you would be kinder to put this poor fellow down now,' was Paul's pessimistic comment.

'No way,' we both said together. 'We know it will be hard, but a little T.L.C should work wonders.' And it did.

Fortunately, we had the winter to work on Pedro before our first guests of the season arrived. We spent hours talking to him while his mange was treated and his hooves pared. He enjoyed his mixed feed and hay, although he had no idea what a hay net was. It amused us to see him shaking it hard and eating the hay as it fell.

This, at least, showed he was quite intelligent, and he was to prove a bright animal with a sense of humour. When later we used him to give rides to guests, he thought nothing of unseating those adults he particularly disliked. Swerving under a low hanging branch, Pedro removed the unsuspecting rider. With children, he was always on his best behaviour. It was the horsey, pony club types he disliked.

When our donkey realised we were his friends, we discovered what a character we had bought. Even his string halt became less pronounced, except when he was upset or nervous. It became a good mood gauge. We had been worried that it would stop him pulling the cart but that was not a problem.

Training a donkey proved quite different from training a pony or horse. Both Ken and I had ridden on trekking holidays. As a teenager, I had been horse mad, working in a stable and driving a governess cart for a neighbour.

I thought we had some idea what to do. In the case of Pedro, however, we suspected that the animal was training us. Bridle and bit went on well from the beginning, but we were never sure if it made much difference, as Pedro went where Pedro wanted to go.

It was the same with learning to pull the trap. We did all the right things in the right order. Harness and blinkers were introduced, though I always had a sneaking suspicion that he peeped round the blinkers.

He happily dragged a log round the field to get used to the feel of a cart, but I think he was just humouring us, as he pulled the cart well from the first; when he wanted to.

As Pedro had been so badly treated we avoided use of a switch, but some discipline was needed. We found that he hated to hear the reins slapped on the breaching, and that used to set him off at a trot. The biggest problem was stopping him. Once he became used to it, he loved to be out in the trap, looking to right and left, not to miss anything. His neck was so strong that had he ever bolted, I would never have held him. When I wanted to stop, I just headed him for the nearest bank or wall.

25

As soon as we were all as roadworthy as possible, I went shopping in the cart. I collected several days' worth of meat, bread, and perishable goods, and it was much easier that balancing it all on a bicycle. When I first started in the guest house, I had no idea how much bread, meat and bacon to buy. I was most grateful to the dear ladies who ran the general grocery, and also to our local butcher. I just had to leave a list of the number of guests and my proposed menus, and they would order my needs. When we had a full house there was no problem, but sometimes extras had to be found for unplanned, casual bookings. On those days, Ken and made do with leftovers.

Ken also found Pedro and the cart useful to deliver our own produce. By this time, we had potatoes, various other vegetables, eggs, dressed poultry, honey, goat's milk and the occasional pound of goat's cheese to sell.

Optimistically, Ken hoped to train Pedro to stand still while he went into a shop or house with the merchandise.

One day, I was in the garden and saw donkey and cart in the field. No Ken. I unharnessed Pedro, gave him a drink and tied him to a post.

I was about to get out my bike to search, when my husband puffed up the drive. 'That bloody donkey!' Ken hardly ever swore, but I could see he was in a state, red in the face and wheezing. I got him his inhaler and heard the story. 'Left him outside the bakery, and took the spuds in; came out and he was nowhere to be seen.'

'Did he undo the tether rope?' I asked innocently.

Ken looked a little embarrassed, 'well, no. I had trained him to stand with the tether trailing.'

'Well, he obviously got bored and came home by himself. What a clever donkey to find his way home on his own, 'I emphasised. Ken just glared at me. After that, Pedro was always firmly tied.

Donkeys have the reputation of being difficult to start. Not so our fellow. As soon as he was untied, our donkey set off at a quick trot. I just had time to make an undignified sprint and jump, grabbing the reins as I vaulted onto the seat of the cart. Then, one day, I discovered he would not move if he was eating something.

From that day, I carried a stale bun or piece of bread with me to give to our crafty donkey as I untied him. He would stand still as I boarded the cart. We were both being well trained.

For a long time we thought unhappiness, illness or loneliness had made Pedro mute, but when he finally decided to speak, there was no half-heartedness about it. Tradition's description of a gentle 'he-haw' was so far from the truth that I wondered if authors of fairy tales and children's books had ever heard a donkey in full throttle. The 'he-haw' is only a small part of the donkey language, and happens when the animal is breathing out. It is the inhalation that is the disconcerting part. Our first demonstration was just as a new batch of guests arrived. It sounded so like the fog horn that we looked out to sea before we realised there was no mist. From that day on, he was as good as a watch dog. He always let us know when someone was near. Unfortunately, he felt he needed practice; usually at dawn or when he wanted moving.

As our fields were unfenced, the goats and donkey had to be tethered on long chains and pegs. It was the general practice on Sark for all grazing animals. Thus, fields were grazed intensively and where the farmer most needed it.

The disadvantage was the need to move the animals several times each day. Pedro was kept on a double length chain with swivels and two pegs; suitable for a bull. Nevertheless, if he decided to come home, up he pulled the pegs and trotted to the kitchen door. Knowing my animal by then, I made sure a tasty crust was available. This saved a lengthy search. A scraping sound on the concrete outside was the first sign that Pedro was loose again. I would hear a soft '*wuffle*' and the doorway grew dark. He was too big to get right through the door.

When this began to happen too often, we realised that more grazing was needed for our goats and donkey. A neighbouring farmer let us rent a field near. As soon as a crop of grass and clover was established, it was a wonderful addition. Bordered by high, mature trees, there was more shelter than in our windblown acres and this was much appreciated in wet and windy weather.

I loved to go early on a spring or summer morning to milk the goats. Everywhere was the song of birds, with skylarks soaring overhead and the cheeky cuckoo shouting his derision nearby.

The distant call of nesting seagulls floated from the cliffs, and rich, green, growing smells mixed with the spicy goat odour. City life could have been on another planet.

26

At first we had no stable for Pedro, but fortunately were able to rent one some distance away. As it was a fair walk, it seemed a good idea to ride. Unfortunately, Pedro did not agree. He did not actually buck us off, but had his own way of dealing with us. He was eleven hands, (big for a donkey), so I had to bend my knees before I could spring up to ride bare back. Watching out of the corner of his lovely brown eyes, our innocent-looking animal stepped sideways, judging to a nicety my point of no return. Many were the times that I landed heavily on my bottom by his side. With a soft 'wuffle' or 'he-haw' he would be off to the other end of the field, but then usually stopped and let me mount, having made his point.

When we eventually had our own stable and the animals were in the rented field, Pedro decided that the road was far too slow a route. Jumping the adjoining banks with the energy of a steeplechaser, he was into his stable and his feed, in record time. If either of us had managed to mount him, it was essential to slide off beforehand, to save a nasty crack from the lintel.

Housing for the goats was a problem, especially as we had acquired 'Mischief', a black and white young goat from a departing resident. We had bought a corrugated iron shed from the Morris', using it mostly for storage of non-perishable goods. However, with just one toilet in the house, Ken and I sometimes used an 'Elsan' chemical toilet placed in one corner of the shed.

When the goats arrived, we moved the stores and divided the shed to accommodate our new livestock. The Elsan was still in the corner near the door, with the partitioned area to the back. This worked well during the day as the goats were usually out in the field. On wet days however, it could be a little crowded, and I lost a few pieces of clothing when I was not paying full attention.

With our growing livestock, Ken and I decided we had to have proper accommodation for them. Being so far from the mainland, building was very expensive. Ken discovered the solution in a newspaper a guest had left behind.

'What do you think about this?' He showed me an advert for prefabricated garden sheds and garages. 'Look, it says it is complete except for the floor. I could do a concrete floor.'

It certainly looked like the answer. 'Apparently you decide how many sections you want. Some are just blank; some have windows and some have doors.'

'How many can you have? We need enough for the goats and donkey; and storage,' I commented. 'Look it says twenty feet is the widest they do; would that be enough?'

We sat down with pad, pencil and ruler that evening, feeling excited. 'I think we could run to the maximum sections.' Ken was becoming enthusiastic. I agreed.

'That will give us a goat section; I'll put a wall between and we can have one door at that end to have access.' Ken nibbled his pencil. 'Then this main part with double doors for Pedro; we'll divide them for stable doors; and then a place for storage of feed.'

'You'll have to make it Pedro-proof.' I pointed out, 'he's like Houdini where food is concerned!'

'Yeh; I'll build a block wall.'

'That still leaves a section at the end nearest the house. Maybe we could create a room for friends, or even us in the summer?' I asked, hoping it was possible. I was becoming tired of our cramped sleeping quarters.

'Well, maybe, though I would like a proper workshop. We can decide later. I'll put a good solid wall between anyway.' I was very much afraid that it would be one more storage place for all those objects that Ken knew would be useful one day. To be fair, he was very handy and good at repairing, but I was sometimes sick of the 'Steptoe' accumulation.

Decision made, Ken then planned the construction, all of which he was going to do himself; he was a builder's son after all. 'The floor in the stable part will have to slope and be channelled, to allow cleaning. The room at the end will need waterproofing and lining.'

'Well, first we have to get permission from the building committee.' I hated to dampen his enthusiasm. To preserve the natural beauty of the Island, all building plans were closely examined. The entire Planning Committee then inspected the site, erecting a pole to show the height and string markers to show the area.

We put in our application, and were told the day of the inspection. The four Committee members walked up the drive accompanied by Pedro's welcome. All were dressed in their best black suits, looking as if they were going to a funeral. I hoped it was not of our plans.

They tramped around in the mud, measuring here and there and eventually erected the pole, and put in place the string markers and pegs. Down they went to the road to see if it was visible, and our hearts sank at the head shaking.

Finally, they finished and accepted a cup of tea and a slice of cake. We sat around for a while, studiously avoiding the topic closest to our hearts. As they were leaving, the Chairman turned to Ken. 'Well, I thought you would have asked.' He grinned. 'I guess it will be OK. You will have to move it a foot nearer the house, but basically it is in order. We'll send you a letter in a couple of days.' We hardly believed a decision had been made so quickly; we were thrilled.

We ordered our new building and the days stretched into weeks. Rain and wind delayed the cargo boat, and we despaired of getting it built before the beginning of season, but arrive it did at last, looking like a gigantic child's construction kit. I hoped to goodness that the instructions had not been lost as there were so many bits. By this time, despite the bad weather, Ken had finished the concrete floors with waterproofed joists embedded, to which he was going to bolt the walls. With his practical mind he set to unravelling the instructions and we were soon ready to start. A few balmy days, forerunner of spring, blessed us, as if apologising for the gales.

In remarkably short time, the building took shape. It was far more satisfying than the traditional construction of frame, walls and finally insertion of windows and doors. Here it was complete; all that had to be added was the glass to the windows. First, one end and a corner section were bolted together, then most of the blank side that would face the boundary bank. As planned Ken divided the double doors into stable doors for Pedro to peer over.

That was fine until he learned how to undo the bolt with his teeth. We really did have trouble keeping him in. Our nosy donkey never appreciated his new home behind the house, as he was unable to see the road and all the interesting things that went on there. It may just have been his curiosity, or his sense of fun, that made him devise ways of escaping. The doors were designed for a garage, and all our hefty donkey had to do was lean on them and they burst open. Eventually we made a double barricade, which foxed him.

Before all that, however, the walls had been erected and bolted to the joists Ken had set in the concrete floor earlier. The roof was the last to go up. Joists were bolted in place and finally sheets of corrugated iron attached to them. The last necessity was to anchor the roof with ropes and blocks, to prevent it stripping off in the next gale.

Just as Ken was up a ladder giving the finishing touches to the roof, he happened to look further up the road to our nearest neighbour's house. It was just visible from the top of the ladder.

'There is something going on at the Brookers', remarked Ken. We saw little of Colonel and Mrs Brooker. They were a reclusive couple.

While abroad in the Army, the Colonel had contracted cerebral Malaria, and occasionally had a relapse, becoming confused and sometimes violent. This was generally controlled by his mouse of a wife, whom he adored. However, we were always a little nervous during these attacks. He thought himself back in the Army and fired his rifle in all directions; often towards Camp Farm which was well in range.

Ken's comment reminded me of a few months ago when I had been involved with the Colonel and his wife. One afternoon, my phone rang and I was amazed to hear Dame Sybil Hathaway's voice. 'I wonder if you could help us, Mrs Davies; we have a spot of bother with your neighbours, the Brookers?' Before I could answer, she continued; 'he's gone a bit odd and won't let anyone in. He's got a machete and is waving it about. The postman saw him and reported it to the Constable.' She sounded unusually hesitant. 'I'm afraid the present constable and the Colonel do not get on.' It was Hap and I could well believe that. 'If we send him in, I am worried what the consequences would be.' She cleared her throat, 'I understand you have been seeing Mrs Brooker recently in your nursing capacity; maybe you could go along and see what you can do.' Of course I agreed.

With trepidation, I had knocked on the door, and the Colonel answered, with machete in hand.

'Er, I have just popped in to see how your wife's leg is.' I held the door open as an escape route. 'That's a huge knife; you got it in India, I think you said.' I knew I was burbling.

'Oh, this, yes I was just giving it a clean; stop for a cupper? The little woman is there; leg's OK now isn't it, Petal.' I breathed a sigh of relief and accepted the cup of tea.

Now, from his vantage point, Ken called down. 'I can see smoke; there certainly is something going on over there. He's firing off his rifle again.' Scrambling down, Ken grabbed the Postman, Paul, who was having a cupper. 'We had better go and see what is happening.'

I waited anxiously, and it was a long time before Ken and Paul returned. I had expected to see the fire engine and tractor go past at any moment, but there was no sign of them. To my, 'what on earth happened?' Paul just grinned and said; 'Ken will tell you all about it, I must finish my round.'

Apparently, the Colonel had taken advantage of the fine weather to burn his rubbish, ignoring the fact that his place was surrounded by highly combustible gorse. 'The silly fellow had set fire to the gorse and the house was ringed with fire.'

'Why didn't he phone the fire brigade?'

'Well, the telephone pole had caught fire too; that's why he fired his rifle. It's a good job I saw the smoke; he's cried 'wolf' too often by firing off that gun at the slightest pretext.'

'So how did you put it out?'

'Luckily his full water tank was outside the ring of fire. We just chopped down the front legs and gallons of water spread all over the blaze,' Ken grinned.

'Lucky for him you were there to help.'

'Well, I think he was more upset with the damage to his tank. Didn't even get a thank you. I'd love a cuppa; any in the pot?'

28

The outside completed, we had to plan the internal divisions of the stable. My admiration grew for my handyman husband. Slow he may be, but he was thorough. Strong walls of breeze blocks were constructed, between goats and donkey. Another partition separated the dry food area, where chicken mash and animal feed were stored in dustbins. Fortunately our greedy donkey never quite managed to remove the lids, to help himself. Pedro so loved his food, but sadly it would cause his death eventually.

We discovered he and the goats loved the small potatoes that we were unable to sell. It was a special treat at the end of the day. Our animals were tethered on long chains and pegs, to conserve grazing. Knowing this delicacy was awaiting them in the stable, there was little fear that they would detour to the vegetable garden after they were released. Each animal had his own bowl and woe betide a trespasser. Pedro usually finished first, and he soon learned that occasionally a trick would produce a few more if we were watching.

One of his favourites was to pick up his bowl in his teeth and hanging his head over the door, would '*woofle*' at us.

When the animals were tethered further afield, it was not practicable to release them to return home on their own.

As the chains were too heavy, Ken made leads with strong nylon rope and clips. I found it was beyond my strength to hold more than one animal intent on the homeward trip. Those left behind set up such a hue and cry that I was sure they could be heard throughout the Island. Often, if the ground was soft, they pulled up their pegs anyway, and galloped past dragging chain and peg behind. At which, the animal I was leading pulled all the more, dragging me with it.

At times like that, the sane civilised life we had left in the city was infinitely desirable. Then phrases like 'self-sufficiency', 'a business of our own', 'calling no-one boss,' crept into my mind. What were a few bruises compared to the joy of living on your own land; growing your own food and hearing the fresh milk spurting into the bucket; or to hold an egg so new that it was still moist?

Originally, we had moved to Sark because we loved it. The guest house was a way to earn a living and be independent. We had also decided at the beginning that as soon as another means of income presented itself we could reduce the number of guests.

There were times when I wondered if it had all become a little out of hand. First there was the guest house, then the smallholding had happened gradually, and now we found we had two full time businesses. Each of these was enough to keep us both occupied, without the other. The strain was beginning to show. I felt it was time to have outside help.

This had always been a bone of contention between us. After three years of good seasons with heavy bookings we were running at a healthy profit but Ken was unwilling to spend too much on outside help. In any case, it was difficult to find a suitable person. In high season, when we needed the most help, all available people were already employed. Some places imported students, but accommodation had to be supplied. We had no spare room. For a while, during the school holidays we employed young Katie, a local girl. She was a pretty and sweet natured girl of thirteen, but had no domestic training and had to be shown everything from scratch. We became good friends, but this was not a solution. So Ken and I carried on, and I cut down on nursing patients when we were very busy.

To make living conditions more comfortable, each room had its own wash basin installed, and we had another toilet connected. Best of all we now had a proper sewage system. For years Ken had battled with what had become an inadequate situation, with the increased number of guests. All the effluent ran into a big tank under the back lawn. When this was full; which was often in high season; the liquids had to be siphoned off. For this Ken used an ancient two stroke pump, which often proclaimed its need for retirement by going on strike. When it did decide to work, there was nowhere to siphon the liquid to, except onto our back field. This was in fact excellent fertiliser, but did not give the sort of odour our guests appreciated.

We found that the middle of the day was the best time for this chore, when guests were out, but it was inevitable that as soon as the smell was the most pungent, a guest would return for something forgotten. It was a relief when we could finally afford a proper soak-away system.

With our guests better catered for, we decided that we also needed something better than a storeroom for a bedroom. Out came the brochures, and we chose a two room chalet-type building with a veranda on one side.

We went through the whole process of planning application and inspection again, but it had no mystery this time. Everything went smoothly and in no time the pieces were delivered. A board floor was included and made Ken's task much easier.

We sited the new building near the back door, for easy access from the kitchen. It was big enough to have a narrow corridor from its front door facing our back door, to one that opened onto a veranda on the far side.

This made two small rooms, but it was bliss not to have to share with toilet rolls and boxes of cornflakes. That was until Ken decided to build more storage shelves high on the three walls not taken by windows.

The other room was used for storage too for a while, but I had plans for its future use.

It was Ken's common sense, and he said, to keep our sanity, that made us postpone trying for a family, as there were so many new projects and activities in our lives. I agreed at first. As six years of our marriage went by, and still Ken wanted to wait, I began to worry. If we left it too long, I felt we would be set in our lifestyle and I was afraid we would never start a family. Realising that I could not have a baby in the middle of the holiday season, the birth would have to be in early winter. This would allow me time to organise my new routine before guests arrived. It would need careful planning, I realised. Wistfully I watched mothers with babies who visited us, thinking how uncomplicated their lives were. I reminded myself that this was the life I had chosen and loved; to be different from the 'common multitude.' It was bound to have its limitations but I would not accept that being childless was one of those limitations.

'Don't you want children then, Ken?' I complained. 'You said you would like two, when we were together in London.'

'Yes, of course, in due time. Don't you think you have enough to do?'

'Well, we have young Katie. She's not so good in the Guest House, but at least she should be able to help with the baby, as she has two younger sisters.' I explained. 'Anyway it would be like one more animal,' I joked, not realising how wrong I was, and how our life was about to change.

I refused to accept Ken's delaying tactics any longer and I begged and begged until he agreed to try for a family. The trying itself was very enjoyable. It was delightful to make time for each other again. For two years we had almost lived parallel lives.

More and more I had taken over the running of the Guest House and chicken business, and Ken spent hours in the garden and with the animals. We were usually so tired at the end of the day that bed was for sleeping only.

For the first few weeks I determined to be patient, and gradually the busy routine took over our lives again. It was the time of year that the postman's visit was most exciting as each mail brought bookings and deposit cheques.

I was in charge of the bookings while Ken re-wrote the brochure and sent off the advertisements to various magazines and the Sark Tourism publication. Just after Christmas each year, he also sent reminder notes to previous guests. Some even left self addressed envelopes as they departed one year, to receive details for the next. This meant that we had many returning guests, which made for a happy household.

With Ken's flair for wording in the advertisements, we were often full at off-peak times in spring and autumn, as well as the high seasons of Easter and summer school holidays. In spring, the Island was Arcadian.

Gentle primroses began to peep from the winter grasses soon after Christmas in a mild year. By April and May the cliffs and verges were glowing with blankets of creamy primroses and brilliant bluebells. Interspersed were red Campion, pink bubbling thrift, white Alexanders like lace doilies, and dark purple dog violets. The trees were beginning to burst into leaf, and the birds sang with relief that the winter was over. It was the best time of year on this small rock settled in the English Channel. The weather could still be wild but stimulating.

It was a tonic to walk on the cliff paths savouring the mingled smells of sea and growing vegetation, exhilarating to the sight of frothy foam and the sound of the nesting gulls.

Later in the year, the freshness disappeared, as dust settled thickly on the roadside from the unsealed roads and the day-trippers' litter fell where flowers once bloomed. High season, the peak time when schools had their longest holidays in July and August, often coincided with the worst summer weather. Strong winds were infrequent, but rainy days were plentiful. The hedgerows that had recently been a blaze of colour were now thick with grass heads, and the leaves lost their bright green of spring. The only flowers still blooming in profusion were sweet honeysuckle and white oxeye daisies.

The heaviness of the August summer days gave a dullness to the Island, the spring sparkle having faded away with the heat of summer. Hundreds of day visitors thronged to gaze at this strange, different, car-less Island, to be wondered at, inspected and talked about afterwards.

One day, I was weeding a flower bed behind the hedge by the road. 'Just think,' I heard a visitor say as she walked by on the road, 'if you lived here, you would not have a worry in the world!'

'Yes,' said her friend, 'but what on earth would you *do* all day?' These visitors never saw the reality, but only the travel book pictures they had paid to see. I felt like popping my head over the hedge and saying, 'The same as you, madam, but rather more of it!'

The guests who stayed with us were different. Many came back year after year, admitting that the thought of their holiday kept them going for the rest of the year. At booking time it was like hearing from old friends.

30

I must have conceived early in those delightful weeks when Ken and I rediscovered our marriage, but I had no morning sickness and felt perfectly healthy, so did not realise it.

One day Ken had gone for a walk with Hugo and Brandy, and I was in the kitchen attending to some letters. Suddenly I heard Pedro making a terrible din in the field behind the house. Dropping everything I rushed out to see our poor little donkey racing round and round on his chain, trying to avoid the teeth of a huge white horse. I recognised Prince, one of our carter Jim's horses. They were always escaping from his badly fenced fields. Having believed for years that donkeys and horses were inseparable and natural companions, I had discovered that some horses simply hated donkeys. This brute was obviously one of them.

Giving no thought to my safety, as I was sure the horse would back off, I rushed out to unclip Pedro and lead him to the stable. I did not know that Prince also hated women.

Suddenly, I felt a hard push in the middle of my back and fell face down on the grass, the horse rearing above me, snorting through his flared nostrils.

Twice I felt a searing, burning pain in my left buttock and thought I had been bitten. Two local boys, taking a short cut through the next field saw it all. They told me afterwards that a hoof had landed close to my spine; further over and it would probably have snapped like a twig.

I lay there for an unbelieving moment, then rolled over and over to escape the huge rearing hooves. Receiving a glancing blow on a shoulder and hip, I scrambled up and staggered to the house, shaking with shock.

The two lads raced to Ken who was just returning and told him what had happened. As he dashed in to the house to see me, the boys chased the horse out of our field. It was then that the tears started, but I could only think of poor Pedro, and insisted that he be stabled first, before I allowed Ken to phone the doctor.

I went to bed, and found I was bleeding. I thought the shock had brought on a period; I realised much later that it must have been a threatened miscarriage.

When the doctor examined me he exclaimed at the developing bruises. 'God, you were lucky! It could have been a lot worse. I'll leave you some painkillers.'

There was no treatment for the gigantic, horseshoe shaped bruise and for months it was with me as a reminder. For the rest of my life there was to be permanent tissue damage. I was unable to sit for long, which did not matter as we were soon into our season of guests.

When we saw Jim he was very apologetic; 'I knew Prince didn't like donkeys but didn't think he would do that. You'd better watch it when you're out with that little cart.' He lifted his cap and scratched his matted hair. 'There's a few other horses don't like 'em. You don't want to cause an accident when the carriages are out.' I almost felt he was blaming me, but could tell by his breath that he had spent his lunch time in the pub. However, he did leave a couple of goose eggs in his old cap, by the gate, next morning.

The confirmation a month later that I was pregnant was enough to take my mind off the nightmares that had woken me sweating since that dreadful day.

31

That season was one of our busiest and most memorable. It was this year that an English couple came with two little children and decided they hated the Island right from the beginning. It was no easy task to keep an eye on lively young children on the rough beaches and steep cliffs of Sark. This couple, with a child of one year and another of two and a half had obviously thought Sark was like Guernsey, with easy access sandy beaches. We could see they were unhappy and were not surprised when they knocked on the kitchen door, after only a few days holiday.

'I think our little boy has German measles. I wouldn't like you to get it; I can see you are pregnant.' The wife would not look me in the eye. 'I think we should leave. Perhaps you will fully refund us as it is for your good.'

'That's kind of you to be concerned. Actually, I am five months on, and it is only dangerous up to about three.' I moved through the kitchen door, 'I am a nurse; perhaps I should have a look?'

'No, no; we should go anyway.'

Reluctantly, we let them go and refunded half their money. It was high season, and we were unlikely to refill at that late date, but we did not want to be unreasonable.

Thinking that was the end of it, we were disturbed to hear from the Sark Hoteliers Association that the young couple had sent a nasty letter about us. Fortunately, their claims were so outrageous and our good reputation was known, so they were not believed. We put this down to experience and discouraged families with more than one small child, in the future.

This year we took up to fourteen guests at a time, having booked them before I became pregnant. My routine was so streamlined by then that it was not too difficult. I had my little helper, Kathy, too.

Everything was going smoothly, but I was beginning to feel a little tired. I needed a rest in the middle of the day, which was unusual for me.

Ken was the one who usually went to bed for forty winks, while I sat in a deck chair in the sun. However, I could not now bear the heat of the sun while I was pregnant, though I had always been a sun worshipper before.

The weather was good that year and we hoped for an 'Indian Summer' as friends were visiting in September.

Late summer into early autumn could be beautiful, and so often the sun was at its best. It was not the hot midsummer scorcher that turned our visitors into lobsters, despite our warnings. With no pollution on Sark to filter the strong rays, we warned our guests that the sun was very strong. Some did not listen and paid the price, becoming painfully burned.

Late summer sun had a gentle, persistent warmth which seeped into everything it touched as if in store for the coming winter. These evenings cast a golden light across meadows, burnishing buttercups and putting a halo round the hydrangea flowers. We seldom went for a walk without taking a container for blackberries, for they grew lusciously everywhere, and the house smelled of the rich spicy aroma of jam.

Our friends came and the weather held, but it was a relief when they left. I was becoming very tired and was growing to quite a size. There were no anti-natal classes on Sark, but reading my midwifery books when I had time helped me assess my condition. I thought all was progressing well, but when I visited the Doctor he told me to rest more, as he was worried that my blood pressure was too high.

When my wedding ring became too tight and I could only wear loose sandals, I had to admit to being a little concerned, but I felt so well. Suspecting that I had toxaemia of pregnancy, the Doctor wanted to send me to hospital after our guests left, to enforce rest, but the decision was soon taken out of his hands.

One day after we closed for the season, I felt well enough to go for a short walk with Ken. It was wonderful to be just the two of us again and have fine weather to enjoy. There were several day trippers about still, and we stopped to talk to a middle-aged woman, not far from our field gate. She was thin and bird-like with a rapid way of talking that made me think of the clucking of my hens.

'Are those your animals in the field over there?' she pointed up the road. 'They are so sweet; especially that adorable donkey, but my, he is a greedy one!' She waved a paper bag. 'He ate all my sandwiches and I wanted to give some to that darling little goat too.' When there were many visitors on the Island the animals were generally kept out of sight.

People wandered all over our land (even picnicking in the fields and on our lawn) and felt it their duty to stuff the animals with all sorts of food. We had thought the danger was over for the year.

With a sick feeling, I asked what had been in the sandwiches.

'Oh, lovely corned beef; I didn't know they ate meat!'

'They don't.' Ken glowered at the woman. 'Meat is a poison to a donkey, blowing them up with gas, and they can't be sick,' he yelled. Brushing past, he hurried towards the field, with me waddling behind. What we saw made me want to kill that stupid woman.

Frothing at the mouth and writhing on the ground, our beloved donkey was in agony. Ken dashed off to phone our vet Paul and I walked as fast as my lump would let me and tried to pull the reluctant animal to his feet. The only hope was to walk the poisonous, intestinal gas through. Ken joined me after phoning. 'He's on his way,' he panted, and managed to get Pedro to his feet.

He started to push Pedro from behind, while I pulled, trying to stop the donkey rolling. That action could fold the intestine in on itself, and it would be fatal. Either that had already happened, or the toxins had been too strong for him, but suddenly Pedro collapsed to the ground, lay kicking for a moment, then died just as Paul arrived.

I could not believe it; it had happened so quickly. Despite my pregnancy, I threw myself onto the still warm body and sobbed as if my heart was breaking, as indeed it was. There would never be another like Pedro, and with him died a little of my love of the life we were leading. A visitor did this. We encouraged visitors onto Sark, and now we had a casualty because of them.

_S**32**

Pedro was not the only casualty. By next morning I was desperately ill. My eyes were so puffy that I could not see properly, and my hands were like sausages. Ken called for the Doctor in panic.

'I don't like this a bit; I can't hear baby's heart,' was his upsetting comment. 'I am going to call the St John Ambulance launch; you just stay in bed young lady!' I felt so restless that I disobeyed and sat outside in the fresh air, trying not to look at the back field.

'I'm sure I'll be OK; just a little rest,' I tried to reassure Ken. 'They surely won't keep me in hospital till I'm due; that's eight weeks yet. I haven't bought any nappies or baby clothes; there was plenty of time.' The Sark ambulance arrived and they insisted on putting me on the stretcher, much to my embarrassment. While the launch and ambulance sped me to the Guernsey Hospital I thought miserably that it was as well there were few baby things if the baby was already dead.

The Doctor at the Guernsey Hospital reassured me. 'You are lucky, Mrs Davies, with a high blood pressure like this, and advanced toxaemia, it is a miracle your baby is still alive.' He looked sternly over his spectacles. 'You must rest and stop worrying, you need isolation and a salt-free diet; must get that oedema down.'

It was all very well to say that, but I could not stop grieving for my Pedro. I would wake in the night and try not to cry, as that would bring the night nurse with tranquilisers. It was after one of these wakeful spells when I had been in hospital a week that I felt a few twinges of pain. As I was still seven weeks away from my expected delivery date I just thought it was the 'false labour pains' that I had read about. I slipped into an uneasy sleep. The pains were still there when I woke, but I told no one, hoping they would go away. By evening I thought I had better call the Nurse. She took one look and called the Sister.

'Goodness, child you are in advanced labour; how long has this been going on?' Not waiting for a reply, she whisked me off to the delivery room. The next few hours are a confusion in my memory. As it was late at night, there was only one nurse on duty.

I was not the only patient in labour; there was another delivery progressing in the unit next door. Alternatively, we were given injections, pills and enemas. One time I was sitting on the toilet and wondered if I was going to pass the baby then and there. 'Don't bear down; don't bear down,' the Sister kept imploring me. I tried to oblige, between vomiting in one bucket and getting rid of the enema in another, but the time came when my little baby would wait no longer. The other mother beat me by a short head, and I could hear her baby crying lustily in the next room. How weak and thin my little premature boy's voice sounded in comparison, and I wished for all the world that mine sounded so well. I was very sad to learn later that the other baby died a few days afterwards, with a collapsed lung.

I was allowed to hold my little boy for a moment before he was put in an incubator. 'Well, Mrs Davies, this baby is only about four weeks early at five and a half pounds weight; you must have got your dates wrong.' It was then I realised how near I had been to losing my son after being trampled by that dreadful horse.

Reluctantly handing my baby back, I asked for a phone. Poor Ken, still on Sark, did not know I was even in labour.

It was then midnight, but with no preamble, I blurted; 'Congratulations, Daddy, you've got a son!' There was a gasp at the other end. 'Are you both alright?' he asked in a weak voice. 'Everything's OK; he's rather small, and they are keeping him in an incubator overnight.' I suddenly missed my sensible husband. 'Can you get Hap or Sam to look after the animals; I mean the goats;' I felt like crying again, 'and come over tomorrow? I miss you, and you must meet your beautiful little son.'

'Oh, dear, the boats are cancelled tomorrow because of the gales!' Exclaimed Ken, 'I'll do my best as soon as I can; sleep tight; and, er ... well done!'

I was not without visitors. The day after our happy event there was a write up in the Guernsey daily. 'Local couple loses donkey but gains a son.' Or words to that effect. Guernsey residents, who had stayed at Camp Farm as guests, sent so many flowers that my corner of the ward resembled a florist's. It was freesia time and I revelled in the tangy perfume, although it made Ken sneeze when he finally arrived.

He was in awe of the tiny scrap and needed persuasion to hold his son. I realised then that he may have been afraid to be a father. An only child, he had never had dealings with infants, but he soon became accustomed to him. Men in those days seldom fed or changed a baby, and Ken was no exception; it was the woman's job.

We discussed names, 'Colin' being a favourite. 'We don't want people to think he's named after the conductor *Colin Davis*,' Ken remarked. We both liked *Roy*, so decided on *Roy Colin*, hoping that he would not have to suffer abbreviations or nicknames when older.

Among my visitors was Ivor, a Methodist minister who had stayed with us several times when he had relieved the Sark Pastor. He had brought his wife June and family that summer, and as June was pregnant too, we had formed a close friendship. Strangely their surname of Davis was similar to ours and Ivor even looked a little like Ken. He was very helpful in bringing nappies and baby clothes, visiting regularly. Later Ivor and June became Roy's Godparents. It was a source of amusement to me that the staff could not decide which was my husband.

I left hospital as soon as I was well enough. There was no health service for Sark residents, so I could not afford to stay a moment longer than necessary. Little Roy had to remain in hospital for another two weeks, to gain weight, so I stayed with Ivor and family who lived near the Hospital.

I went in every day to feed my tiny baby, but as Roy was so sleepy I had to abandon breast feeding after the first few days.

$\mathbf{A}$t last, the wonderful day arrived when we could return to Sark. Ken came over to collect us. For once the weather was kind and the late October sun was a blessing. I had been worried that Roy would chill after the warm hospital cocoon.

As our taxi approached the quay, I was pleased to see it was the cargo boat which also took a few passengers, doing the trip that day. The cabin on this boat was smaller than the regular boat used in the busy holiday season, but it was easily reached on the forward deck. I had worried about carrying a new baby down into the enclosed smoky cabin on the other boat.

Suddenly I heard the unmistakable 'he-haw' of a donkey. I thought I was going mad. Grabbing Ken's arm, I was surprised to hear him laugh. 'That's let the cat out of the bag; well, the donkey, really!' He led us towards the quay, where they were loading the last items before the passengers were allowed to board. 'Look there's Pedro Mark 2.' He pointed to a canvas sling suspended above the cargo hold. With legs stuck out at each corner and tail swishing behind, the donkey was shouting his discomfort to the world.

My feelings were a little mixed, but I knew Ken had done it for me, so tried to be appreciative. I felt I had enough to do with a tiny baby who would need feeding every three hours; and I felt so weary all the time.

It was different being at home with a baby to look after; a baby who cried so much. I felt so inadequate. I had thought that motherhood would come naturally; being a nurse it was assumed that I would know what to do. I fed him; he cried; I changed him; he cried; I bathed him and he screamed even more. The only time Roy was quiet was when he was asleep. Fortunately after a few weeks he slept several hours during the night.

A copy of the *Dr Spock* book became my bible, but I discovered this was one thing we could not do by the book. I realised Roy was a colicky baby; he had all the symptoms described. He used to curl up and yell after his feeds. He even had his special 'crying times' at four in the afternoon. No matter what I did, we had three solid hours of yelling. Lying the little baby tummy down on a warm hot water bottle and gently rubbing his back helped a little.

I became very tense and could not eat. Everywhere I went I could hear my baby crying in my head. For the first time in my life I could not cope and it frightened me. There were times when I felt I would do anything to stop the crying. It was easy to understand how babies could be battered. Thank goodness that Ken was around to take his little son when I could stand it no longer.

To make it worse, mother-in-Law visited. Reserved by nature, she could not understand my distress. Surprisingly Roy was more settled with her, and I began to feel it was all my fault that he cried so much. Perhaps it was. I had heard that the bond between a new baby and its mother is made close by hormones that stay in the mother's body long after birth. This is nature's way of protecting the defenceless. The bond is very close and emotions pass between mother and baby by an invisible chord, as vital as the umbilical cord. My distress was passing to Roy and so back to me. It was not until much later I realised that the toxaemia had upset my hormone balance and was causing clinical depression.

In the meantime the holiday season was on us again, and somehow I had to cope with guests and all the work involved.

I realised I needed medical help. I was referred to a specialist, who diagnosed depression and put me on Valium and Tryptanol; two potent anti-depressants.

It helped me get through the season, but how I managed was a miracle. All the joy had gone from life; everything seemed pointless. Even the new Irish donkey Shamus failed to cheer me.

One day I went for a walk on the cliffs on the nearby headland, while Ken looked after Roy. I just had to get out of the house. My wanderings took me to the very edge of a cliff and I stood, looking down at the swirling seas below. The gulls were spinning and gliding against the steep cliffs, making me dizzy. It would be so easy to slide down to the foaming waves below; they looked so soft and inviting but I knew the hard rocks were just below the surface, and the little sense I had left reminded me that I may end up as a cripple. I drew back in horror; how could I forget Roy and Ken, who needed me? I had to sort this problem; now.

That was a turning point. Gradually I eased myself off the antidepressants and started reading my nursing books and magazines.

One article dealt in detail with toxaemia and its after effects. 'Often the system does not right itself without intervention. Sometimes a hormone supplement may be needed,' was one comment. Could that be my problem? I had noticed that my bouts of depression were cyclical, being worse every two weeks. I went to see a gynaecologist.

'Yes, indeed Mrs Davies it could well be. I understand you had severe toxaemia of pregnancy. It does sometimes upset the natural rhythm,' she smiled encouragingly. 'Look we'll try you on this high progesterone contraceptive pill for a while.' I opened my mouth to say I did not want a contraceptive pill, but then the thought of becoming pregnant again scared me.

Sure enough, in a few months my depression was much less. I began to enjoy my son, who was by then nearly a year old.

I realised I had lost a vital part of his development. Strangely it seemed to have done him no harm, except that he had two small inguinal hernias. Whether that had been from the crying or partly the reason for it, I would never know. It was true that his father had had a similar problem when he was younger. Roy eventually had two operations, but fortunately they passed without problems.

I never regained the delight and enthusiasm for our projects. My usual bounding good health was slow to return and I tired easily.

Another year passed and Roy grew in health and happiness. From being a sickly crying baby, as a toddler he was a delight. His nature was naturally easy going and sunny and has remained so for the rest of his life. Stubborn though. Once I asked him to put his toys away. Half an hour later I returned to the lounge where he had been playing. Toys were still scattered everywhere. 'Roy!' I said sternly, 'I told you to put your toys away.'

'Did, Mummy; didn't say not to get them out again.' There was no answer to that logic.

One day after a trip to Guernsey, Ken dropped two library books on the table. There were magical pictures of mountains and beaches on the cover.

'I was just thinking, Roy is getting nearly to three, it won't be long before he goes to school.' He gave me a frank look, 'I think this life is getting you down a bit; well I could do with a change for a year or two, as well.

I looked at the front of the first book. 'New Zealand!' I exclaimed.

'Well, if we want to have a look at it, we'd better do it before Roy is five.'

I looked at the two special men in my life, and felt the familiar surge of excitement returning.

'Why not?' I said.

****

This is the second memoir by this author, telling of her experiences of life on the little Feudal Island of Sark. In this, she has returned on her own to live with 'the love of her life' Peter, and to work as the Island's nurse after the breakdown of her marriage to Ken

****

MY LIFE ON SARK

BOOK 2

SO YOU RETURNED TO SARK

CHRIS DAVIES CURTIS

1

I could hardly hear my mother's voice on the telephone. There was a ringing in my ears and my heart was pounding.

'Just a minute, Momma, read that again. I don't understand. Ken and I had agreed I was coming back to New Zealand to live separately and try and sort things out. We can't go on as things are.'

There were tears in her voice when she read from my husband's letter. 'Oh Chrissie! He says; "Tell Chris that unless she comes back as before, not to come back at all." What are you going to do?'

The ringing had stopped and I felt I was floating. I could not hear the Airport noises nor see the people hurrying past the phone kiosk. There was an artificial stillness in me and I heard a voice . . . my voice . . . saying calmly. 'Well I'm just not going back to New Zealand, then. I must sort myself somehow. I will contact you when I know what I am doing: must go: don't worry.'

I hung up and turned to Peter who had been waiting patiently. He stretched out his hand and gripped my arm. 'Are you OK? You're as white as a sheet!'

'I'm fine thanks.' The calm was still with me, and I felt as light as a feather. 'I'm not going back.'

'What?'

'I will never sort myself out if I go back to New Zealand just now. For all his words, Ken will not accept we are finished if I am there.'

'What about Roy?'

'He'll be O.K. I'll have to go back when I am sorted. He'll be off to University soon: he is nearly seventeen.' I had my first pain of indecision. My beloved son; how would I tell him his mother was leaving the family?

'It's not for ever:' but as I said it I knew that I was changing all our lives irrevocably.

Peter's practical voice brought me back to reality. 'We'd better go to the Airline desk and see if we can get your suitcase back.'

I was beginning to shake with shock at the enormity of what I had decided to do. Yet in my heart was a deep relief that at last I was able to take some action. There had been too many years of living parallel lives with little warmth on either side of our marriage.

The Airline staff were most sympathetic. Peter explained to them that I had to cancel my flight due to an emergency. I suppose they could see from my face that I was upset.

'You're lucky Mrs Davies: your case has not gone out to the plane yet. We can open your return ticket. It will be valid for a year, but you may have to pay a little more if the fares go up.' I nodded, hardly able to think beyond the relief of not having to go back just yet, and to be able to spend more time with my Peter.

We sat in the cafeteria at the Airport, trying to make plans.

'What will you do: where will you go? Will you go to Yorkshire to stay with your parents?'

Gradually the numbness left me. I had to think.

'No: Ally said I could stay with her in the farmhouse. She said I should stay longer and sort myself. You remember Alison?'

Peter and I had visited my old school friend in her village near Cheltenham, when we had rented a cottage near her for a few days at the beginning of my holiday.

My father was very ill with Parkinson's disease and I had taken six week's leave from my job as a rural district nurse in New Zealand to spend some time with my parents. I also wanted to see Peter again.

Ken and I had known Peter and his wife, Marjorie when we both ran guest houses on the tiny feudal Island of Sark in the British Channel Isles. Peter and I had remained good friends and written to each other after Ken and I moved to New Zealand. We had both unburdened ourselves as our marriages fell apart, each seeking from the other comfort and support. Then we met again on one of my trips to visit my parents, taking Roy to see his grandparents.

We fell in love. We had not planned for anything like that to happen. I had returned to Sark for a week to catch up with old friends while Roy stayed with Ken's mother in London. By this time Peter had moved to a small cottage in the garden of the place he had bought to be away from the guests, while Marjorie stayed in the main house. I called to visit and was devastated to see this strong man needing a shave, with buttons off his shirt and with an unkempt appearance. My heart went out to him, and stayed there. By the end of the week he admitted he had loved me for some time but neither of us saw any future together. I was still trying to make my marriage work at that time.

We continued to write when I returned to New Zealand. Now the letters were often more intimate and by the time we met again we knew somehow, sometime we had to be together. We were going to wait until Roy was at University, but now, suddenly everything had changed. I was on a rollercoaster to a major change in my life.

2

Peter had been planning to stay with his daughter and her family in Gloucester for a few days before returning to Sark. I had known his two daughters and son a little in the early days but as they went to boarding school in Guernsey, the nearest large Island, I had seen little of them.

'I've just given Lyn a ring and told her a little of what has happened . . .' I opened my mouth to comment but Peter continued . . . 'no, I didn't say much, just that you had had to stay on longer. She knows about us, you know.'

I felt my face turning red. 'I am not sure there is an 'us' yet. I need to find myself first.'

He took my hands in his. 'I think we need to be together; but I agree you must have some time on your own: but don't take too long to make up your mind.' With that he pushed my bag towards the exit and the hired car and I walked beside him.

Lyn and her husband made us welcome, but they had no spare bedroom.

The two children had to share and I had one room while Peter slept downstairs on a sofa bed.

'And no pussy-footing up and down the stairs in the night!' She said with a twinkle in her eye. I managed to get back to my bed just before the family stirred in the morning.

The next few days were best forgotten. I had to make the dreaded phone call to Roy and of course to Ken. They both took it quietly, and Roy showed a maturity beyond his years.

'I knew you were unhappy Mum. I could hear you crying sometimes; and when you moved to the spare room, well I knew there was something wrong.'

'Will you be O.K?'

'I was going to tell you when you came back. I've got a girlfriend from our class at school; in fact we have been dating for a year or more . . .'

'Roy that's wonderful!' I had been concerned when my son had shown no signs of going out with girls. I even had a worrying thought that he may prefer his own sex.

'There's just one thing, Mum, she's in a wheelchair. She has spina-bifida.'

'Well, that's O.K. isn't it? Is she, er, alright?'

'Of course. She's one of the brightest in the class.'

'That's good. I'm glad for you. I think I'd better be going. I'll write when I have somewhere to stay.'

'Mum. . .'

'Yes?'

'Don't worry. Will you be O.K?'

I choked back my tears. How I was going to miss my only child.

'I'll be O.K. I have Peter.'

I rang off and took a deep breath. The first hurdle was over: now I had to find somewhere to live and then get a job.

The day after my dramatic decision, Peter and I visited my friend Ally. She did not seem surprised as we rolled up to the old Cotswold stone farmhouse in our hired car. The rambling building was situated right in the middle of the village, opposite an ancient eleventh century church. As my friend opened the solid oak door, a clarion of bells rang out from the square church tower. My friend and I stood there grinning at each other, speech being impossible, as the joyful music rang and then Ally gave me a big hug.

'Well, I see you have taken my advice, Chrissie.' She gave Peter a kiss on his cheek and pulled us into the warm kitchen, heated by an 'Aga' stove. Over steaming cups of coffee and home-made cake I asked if her offer still stood of a room for a few weeks.

'Of course! When do you want to move in?'

'Er, tomorrow?'

'Come and see the room. You'll need to tidy it up a bit.' Through rambling corridors and up innumerable flights of stairs, we eventually arrived on the top floor, at what was going to be my home for rather longer than I had expected.

A huge bed dominated, with basic furniture wedged in where it would fit. There was a tiny wardrobe but as I only had one suitcase of clothes, it would be enough. The small window which nestled deep into the stone wall looked directly at the church and churchyard.

'How often does the church clock strike?'

'Every third hour: through the night as well.' Ally's grin did nothing to comfort me.

I became so used to the bells I hardly heard them after a while. The only problem was when someone phoned on the third hour it was impossible to talk for several minutes. The farmhouse had a Grandfather, a Grandmother and a Granddaughter clock which were tuned to strike one after the other, following the church clock. Peter and I soon learned to avoid phoning one another at those times in the ensuing months.

That evening Peter and I discussed the immediate future.

'You'll need transport. What say we go and find something reasonably cheap tomorrow?'

We bought an old Fiat Strada that went well but was a little battered. It was a game little car and did well for the time I needed it.

Peter lent me the money as I had little left until I found a job. I had planned to transfer money from my New Zealand account to one I had kept in Sark. However I was in for a shock. The New Zealand account was a joint one and fearing that he would not have enough for himself and Roy to live on, as we had lived off my salary, Ken had withdrawn everything, including my share. I was nearly destitute. My need for a job became urgent.

I had sent a letter to my district nursing department in New Zealand, saying I had decided to stay on in England

for an indeterminate time. I resigned and apologised for
any inconvenience: I was not sure if I would get a
reference and so would be seeking a nursing job without
one.

With a reasonable climate, level streets and many
excellent shops, Cheltenham is a popular retirement town.
So, there are also many private nursing homes.

I set to the next day working my way through the
telephone directory. Not having a reference did not seem
too much of a disadvantage: the main problem was that I
was not sure how long I would be in the town.

One fact in my favour was that the holiday season was
beginning and nurses were wanting to book leave. At the
fourth Nursing Home I was offered a temporary job as a
relief Sister.

'Can you work shifts, and some nights Mrs Davies?'

Yes, I could: I had nothing much else to do and knew
few people in the area so I was not anticipating a social
life.

It was agreed I could have an occasional weekend off
as I was longing to spend some time with Peter again. He
had returned to Sark, but we planned to meet as often as
we could.

I entered a strange half-life.

I had believed when I made the decision to stay on in
England that I would go back to New Zealand after a
while, to live on my own till Ken and I could come to
some arrangement.

As I spent time with Peter it became more and more
difficult to think of a life without him even for a year or
two. When he was not with me I could still feel his
presence. When he phoned, I would dash to answer,
breathless as a teenager with her first love.

Ally was a great friend in need, absorbing me into her
life effortlessly. We had been good friends at school, and
I had spent many happy hours at her father's farm. Now
she and her husband had their own farm and she was a
busy shepherd, with a prize herd of breeding sheep.

On one occasion I went with her to a local show in a neighbouring town.

'I'm a bit worried about the big ram. He's a randy old devil and if there are any ewes on heat, he'll be hard to handle.'

While I was a district nurse in New Zealand I had become interested in complementary medicine and homeopathy in particular. I had used Bach Flower Rescue Remedy sometimes in stressful circumstances and remembered being told it was effective in calming animals.

'Well it won't do any harm.' Ally was obviously not convinced, until she admitted on the way home that she had never seen the ram behave so well. 'What was that stuff called, Chrissie. . .I'll get a bottle full!'

It was one small thing I could do to repay her kindness.

Church opposite Ally's House

3

I had forgotten how bewitching early summer could be in England, especially in the rural Cotswolds. The fragrance in the air was intoxicating: a mingling of wildflowers, blossoms and lush growing greenery. The dawn was so early that it seemed the sun had hardly set before the birds awoke to announce the new day with a joyful chorus. Wood pigeons cooed gently as a background to the trill of blackbird and thrush, with the strident cuckoo shouting his defiance above them all.

I had not realised how I had missed it all in the brasher, sub-tropical vibrancy of New Zealand. Now it acted as a balm to my tumbling emotions. I allowed myself to slip into my new life, avoiding making a decision about my future. It was enough to drive the old car to work along a country road: to park under the lush green trees and spend the day tending to my elderly patients. Back at the farmhouse I often cooked the evening meal for Ally and her husband. I enjoyed the luxury of using an Aga and learned how to stack a dishwasher: a novelty for me.

We would sometimes sit outside with a glass of wine as the days got warmer. Over the constant sound of cooing doves, I would have one ear listening for the frequent phone calls from Peter: my heart skipping a beat when I heard his familiar voice.

I realised that I would have to make a decision. Ken was beginning to talk of separation: Roy was studying for exams, and although he was missing me, accepted the situation. I convinced myself that if I returned to New Zealand it would aggravate things again.

It did not take much persuasion on Peter's behalf for me to decide. We had managed to have a weekend together in Guernsey, but I had not visited Sark during my time in England.

I loved the tiny feudal island where Ken and I had run our guest house and smallholding for about seven years, before touring New Zealand for two years and then finally emigrating there in 1976.

When we had left the Island, we had leased our house and business for ten years. There were eighteen months to run at 'Camp Farm', and then we would have to decide what to do with the cedar-shingle house and two acres of land.

'I think I should visit Sark and talk to the tenants.'

'Yes, Chrissie, I think it is time for you to come back to Sark. I want you to come and live with me, but I can't offer you marriage, you know that.'

Many of the laws of this strange little Island were feudal. It had its own government, the 'Chief Pleas' and head of state, the 'Seigneur'. Some of the constitution had been brought up to date, and the system worked well. However there were still some peculiarities. One was that there was no mechanism in place to divorce a couple who both lived on the Island. One of them would have to leave the Island for a year and a day. If they did that, then they may possibly run into some residential problems on their return.

'What about Marjorie and your son, David?'

'Marjorie says you are welcome to me. She says you have always been her friend.' Peter said this with a wry expression.

'It is so bizarre. It all seems so unreal.' I was far from happy about living 'out of wedlock' but there was no alternative if we wanted to be together.

'Well it is very real, Chris. If you feel you can't face the gossip … and you know there will be some, maybe we should get a little cottage somewhere else.'

'I couldn't do that to you. You love the Island and the life there and David has just returned from Agricultural College. Didn't you say he had managed to get a lease on the 'Old Farmhouse?'

'Yes, well I was hoping to give him a bit of a hand in the renovations, but. . .'

'I love Sark too. No ...' I made one of my snap decisions: 'I shall come back for a trial period. At least if they are gossiping about me they will give someone else a rest!'

So began my return to the little Island set in the English Channel just off the French coast, which I had first moved to in 1966. There had been some change in that time. Tourism was still the main source of income but with the advent of computers and the blossoming of the finance industry, Sark had become a tax haven. Companies had discovered the advantage of registering in this Income-Tax free Island. There were many company directorships for grabs, and large incomes could be earned by the less scrupulous, for little effort. Others did work very hard with the more honourable companies. Unfortunately, the few who did not were beginning to give a bad name to the Island in what was beginning to be called 'The Sark Lark.'

Peter told me all about the changes in the population, during the years of our previous exchange of letters. The older indigenous 'Sarkese' were dying out, although there were still families able to trace their ancestry back to the first 40 settlers, or *Tenants* who had arrived on the small, inhospitable island 400 years ago. The English residents of the time I lived on Sark were mostly 'ex-colonials:' people who had been forced to leave the diminishing English colonies. They saw the life in the British Channel Islands preferable to returning to England. However they found the proud descendants of Norman France not of the same calibre as the servants they had left behind. The Sarkese did not kowtow to the newcomers' every wish, and resented being called by their Christian names without permission. The ex-colonials formed 'cocktail' and 'lunch' groups, which we working English had not been invited to attend.

The population, still at around 500, now comprised partly of younger workers, visiting for the summer season. Some were employed at one of the five hotels: others drove the many horses and carriages for visitors. Several stayed and married local people while others opened guest houses and self-catering units.

The Sark I returned to was different in many ways to the one I had left ten years previously. I had nightmares while in New Zealand that the Island would become like everywhere else. I was delighted that there were still no cars allowed and that there were no tar-seal roads. The wild beauty of the cliffs and hedgerows and unspoiled leafy valleys remained, although some modernisation had taken place. The boat service had improved, with the addition of two faster launches, making trips to the bigger neighbouring island of Guernsey more frequent. The electric supply service was mainly by an Island generator, and there were now few places that produced their own, to the peace of the surrounding houses. Fishermen still put out their lobster and crab pots, but their wares found their way to the hotels, and it was almost impossible to get fresh fish from them.

The hotels and guest houses had modernised. Visitors were no longer satisfied with outside toilets and jugs and bowls in the rooms, a common situation when I had run our guest house. Now they expected en-suite, or at least a well appointed shared bathroom. The standard of catering had also changed. Each hotel had an excellent restaurant for non-residents as well as guests, and there were other independent restaurants.

It had become normal to dine out and socialise on a regular basis. I was going to find life with Peter on Sark very different.

4

When I returned to Sark in the summer of 1984, we did not have a place to live. Then Marjorie suggested we use the little cottage in the garden of the place she and Peter had bought, that Peter had been living in for some time.

Although Peter had said his wife had declared that she did not want to live with him anymore, I could not really believe she would be so welcoming. It was an unreal situation.

Eventually we became an odd trio, often going out together to public functions and Peter gained a certain notoriety with his 'two wives.' Marjorie was to become a frequent visitor to us for meals, especially when their two daughters were on holiday on Sark. We also sometimes helped her with her garden and decorating.

It did not take me long to decide that my future was with Peter on Sark. I soon fell again under the spell which had bewitched me all those years ago when I had first visited this unique place. The pace of life was different: the challenges of daily existence were immediate: you survived or gave in by your own efforts, though you lived as a part of a community. Everyone had the same dependency on the weather: a concern if the Island's lifeline, the boat service, was cancelled and a knowledge that cycling or walking were the only options of transport.

As the UK National Insurance Scheme did not extend to the Channel Islands, there was no sickness or unemployment benefit. It was essential to have private health insurance. There was seldom anyone unemployed: the roads had to be maintained in winter and in the summer staff were needed in the hotels and shops. There was always the odd job or bit of decorating to be done if someone did need employment.

I went to see the young couple, now with three little boys, who had leased our old 'Camp Farm.' My reception was not very friendly and I was surprised. Despite a higher offer when we had advertised the business to lease, we had chosen them as being Channel Islanders. We felt they would be more at home with island life.

'You never answered our letter when we wrote to say we wanted to buy the place.' They said when I visited them.

I knew nothing of this and realised Ken had never discussed it with me, but the young couple did not believe me. I think they never forgave me, as they were not very friendly for the whole time I knew them.

However, as they were planning to build their own house, eventually they agreed to let me buy back the remaining part of the lease. I now had Camp Farm and we had somewhere to live: or so we thought until we went on a tour of inspection.

'Just look at this.' Peter pushed open a window and it swung out on rusted hinges, nearly falling into the flower bed below. 'And there are leaks in two of the bedrooms. Is this the same roof as when the house was built in 1946?'

I assumed it was. The old cedar 'Colt' house had been built just after the war, not long after the German occupying force had been removed when the Island had been liberated. We had built a new entrance porch, but apart from that, little had been done besides repainting.

'It will need new windows and a roof, and I wouldn't be surprised if rain hadn't leaked from the window frames to the studs underneath.' Peter shook his head. 'Be better to knock it down and start again.'

'Well, it's not all mine yet anyway. Ken still owns half.'

I had been in communication with Ken, and we were reaching an agreement about our separation. He seemed much happier since Peter had offered to give a quarterly financial settlement to help Roy in his schooling and expenses. Peter's only stipulation was that Roy was to give a breakdown of how the money was spent, which he was happy to do.

Finally we came to an agreement that Ken would relinquish his half of Camp Farm and I would sign over my half of the property we had in New Zealand. The value was not equal so I also had to give Ken a substantial cash payment. I was able to do that as Peter had purchased a half of Camp Farm. Peter and I would then jointly own the property, but it was not a simple procedure under Sark law. Ken and I had first to sell it to a third party and then Peter and I had to buy it back. My solicitor was engaged to be the intermediary and so finally I could 're-purchase' my own property. Another complication was the payment of the *tresieme*. This was a type of 'duty', of a thirteenth part of any purchase price added onto the value of a freehold property, which Camp Farm was. Ken and I had already paid a *tresieme* when we bought the property in 1965 and I had visions of paying a second time. However fortunately there was legislation to cover that eventuality.

Finally the legal details were sorted and at last we could plan for the future. The problem was where to live while we re-built Camp Farm. The cottage we were in was only two rooms and a tiny bathroom.

Peter's son David came to our rescue. The shy young boy I had known had grown into a handsome, delightful young man. Qualifying well from an agricultural college in England it had always been his dream to return to the Island he loved and have his own farm there, but it was not an easy goal to achieve. Most of the land belonged to one of the original 40 'tenements,' when the Island had been divided 400 years ago by the first ruler, or *Seigneur*. These still remained intact and consisted of several houses and fields. The sale price was far beyond the reach of all but the wealthy. It was possible to rent or lease buildings and fields, and it was for one such neglected farmhouse that David had managed to buy a lease.

'You can come and use some of the rooms in the 'Old Farm' if you don't mind roughing it a bit. Perhaps we can come to some agreement?'

So began my new life on Sark. It was still strange to have no real home, but wonderful to be with Peter each day. I missed Roy very much and had to be careful not to try and 'mother' David. I thought he was amazingly mature to accept the odd situation he found himself in: his father living with another woman while his mother accepted the situation. I suspect it was for that very reason that David and his sisters accepted me eventually. I was truly fond of Marjorie and had known her quite well when I had lived on Sark before. She was of a quiet and retiring nature and I had often wondered how she coped with Peter's ebullient, fun-loving extrovert personality.

Peter had admitted in his letters that he and Marjorie had been living parallel lives much as Ken and I had been. He had thought of leaving, but while his children were growing up and going through tertiary education he had shelved any plans.

Both Peter's daughters lived not far from where I had been working in the Cotswolds. They were both married and I had met them a few times while I was there. Naturally they were reserved with me, especially the younger, Ann, who was close to her mother. Gradually we all got to know each other, and when they realised Marjorie accepted the situation, I was generously accepted by all of Peter's children. Over the years I grew to love them and their eventual children. I was delighted to have 'a second family.'

5

My acceptance by people on Sark took a little time. I had kept in touch with my goddaughter's family. Valerie. . .Val for short, was now a young woman. I was sad that I had missed her younger years, remembering my delight when I had delivered her in an emergency, at her parent's home all those years ago. Her mother Annie and grandmother May still ran the general grocery shop in the village. Annie's husband Sam and son Jerry worked with my old sparing friend Hap in their farm, and Louise, Val's sister was showing an aptitude for making pottery, under the tuition of her ex school-teachers.

They were still my 'Sarkese' family and welcomed me whenever I called in to the shop for a cuppa. It would not be long before I became much more involved with this hard-working family.

In the infrequent letters from Val while I was in New Zealand, I learned of the dreadful accident that befell her grandfather, Hap, a year or so previously. He had been leaning over an unguarded bailer, when his coat caught in the machinery, tearing his left arm almost from his body. It had to be amputated. If that was not enough, the shock aggravated a latent family predisposition to diabetes and hypertension. He did not take kindly to medication and often refused his treatment.

My friendship with this outspoken difficult Sarkee had been unusual in my days of running the guest house. Sarkese and English did not usually form a friendship but we delighted in sparring with each other, neither giving in to the other.

On my return I was pleased that our friendship had not changed, but I was genuine in my concern for the possible effect of his stubbornness. As a trained nurse I knew what the outcome could be.

'I can't be bothered taking all that rubbish, eh.'

152

'It's not rubbish. It is to stop you having a stroke or worse.'

'Don't care. I'll be out of it then.'

'Huh, well you may not. You may end up paralysed.' I did not know how prophetic my words would prove to be.

Peter and I settled in the Old Farm and I offered my services as a private district nurse again on the Island. While running the guest house and smallholding, I had worked with the only doctor on Sark. There was no official district nurse, but usually a retired nurse living on the Island would offer her services when needed. I found that the woman who had been doing some work was only too happy to let me take on patients. I was delighted to be nursing again, having spent the majority of my working life caring for people in their own homes. I was to continue for the rest of my time on Sark, working with the doctor and even acting as locum doctor for up to 24 hours if he needed to leave the Island briefly. It was this service that was to draw me back into the Island community. As someone once said; 'Well, we don't know when we might need you!'

I was to be grateful for the seven years as rural district nurse in New Zealand. I learned a great deal about maximum nursing care in the home, and in teaching relatives how to become experienced carers. I was soon to need all my expertise in training my 'Sarkese family.'

The call came early one morning. 'Auntie Chris,' I could hardly recognise Val's voice; 'it's Pop: he's in hospital in Guernsey; he had a stroke in the night and he's paralysed all down his right side. Mum's over there now.'

'I'll come round.'

I offered what support I could in the next few days and helped a little in the shop until Annie came back.

'He hasn't had another and the doctor over there says he may be over the worst, but his right side is all paralysed and he can't talk . . . well except to say 'terna buggre!' Annie looked determined. 'Chris, I want to bring him home. They say he could go on like this for some time, or he might just have another. They won't let me bring him home though, unless I have nursing help. . . do you think. . .' I did not wait until she finished.

'Of course he must come home, and I will help as much as I can. We'll need to get some equipment from the St John's in Guernsey.'

Plans were made over the next few days. The family lived in two adjacent houses, with the shop and some accommodation in one and the main living area in the other. The trouble was that there was no bathroom in the house with the shop.

'We could turn the back storeroom into a bathroom and have Hap in a bedroom off the kitchen. We will then be able to keep an eye on him and he would hear what was going on.' So this is what was done. Sam and Jerry were handy men and it took no time at all installing a bathroom and widening the doorway.

I had connections with the St John Ambulance and Rescue in Guernsey who had an excellent equipment hire service. Soon I arranged to have a hospital bed, ripple mattress (to prevent bed sores), a commode, mechanical hoist and a bath seat sent to Sark. Now all we needed was Hap.

When my friend arrived I was shocked by the change in him. I was expecting the physical change, but the spirit had gone too. I knew this often happened and determined I would get the fight back.

'Well you old bugger, I warned you this might happen! Well I've got you at my mercy now.' There was a glint in his eye, and he muttered . . .'T.t.t.er' and that was the beginning.

He was a mess. With his left arm missing and the right side paralysed, there was only movement in the left leg. A bedsore cut deep into his right heel and there was no control of natural functions. He had a catheter in to relieve his bladder and needed help with everything else. He was a challenge, but I had been used to this sort of case.

Annie was an apt pupil. She had been giving Hap his insulin injections before the stroke, and now he had no choice but to swallow his other medication. I showed her how to roll her father over and sit him up on the edge of the bed, ready to wrap the sling harness round him for the hoist. Hap was not much help and tried to resist till I gave him a good talking to. 'You can be bloody-minded and be difficult and make life hard for everyone, or you can co-operate. Either way we are just as stubborn as you, and we will win.' Hap's power of speech was still limited and consisted of two patois swearwords; 'Terna buggre', which did not need translation, and an explosive 'Te-te-te.' He never said anything else in all the time I helped with his care, and refused speech therapy. But I have never heard so many different ways of saying those few syllables.

At first I visited several times a day. There were many things for the family to learn. They all did their share, but it was on Annie's shoulders that the main burden fell. We soon managed to get Hap into the bath on the special seat, using the mechanical hoist. It was a Godsend as we could not have managed the heavy man without. For a while he was in bed all day, and the ripple mattress also was essential to stop bedsores. A small transformer pumped air into alternate cells in the plastic over-mattress, thus relieving the patient's weight on any one spot every few minutes.

The existing bedsore on his right heel was a problem. As a diabetic, the skin healed badly and there was a danger of gangrene. Fortunately I had been using a wonderfully healing liquid while in New Zealand. It was made from marigolds, called calendula and was known to aid cleansing of wounds and to promote healing. By packing Hap's deep sore twice a day with gauze moistened in this magic liquid, it healed completely.

The other big problem was the catheter. As the stroke had affected natural functions, it was necessary to have a catheter in place permanently.

Blockages were frequent and excruciatingly uncomfortable for Hap. This often happened in the middle of the night and required swift attention. Sometimes it was possible to unblock it, but more often than not it was necessary to re-catheterise. The first few times the doctor attended, but sometimes he would be out on a call, and poor Hap would be writhing in agony by the time help came.

'I know female nurses are not supposed to catheterise men,' I said to the doctor after one of these occasions, 'which in my mind is ridiculous . . . but I was trained to do it on my district in New Zealand. Would you let me do it next time?'

'Och, aye,' he was a lovely Scotsman, 'I dinna see why not; I'll watch ye the first time, for the record, ye ken.'

So, I took that on, and became quite expert at the most difficult catheterisation I had ever had to do.

Each day when it was not a bath day, Annie and I would wash Hap. On one of these occasions, a month or so after he returned to Sark, I was lifting his right leg up and it jumped out of my hand.

'Hap, you moved your leg!' I could hardly believe it. I gave him a big hug which brought on an explosion of '*Te-te-te's*'. 'You know, we will get you walking if it kills me!'

We did. It took a lot of effort by all of us. He never managed by himself, but with Annie in the right supporting the bad side and me on the left, he did manage to walk up and down the kitchen. As there was no arm on the left to hook mine into, I had to support him with both my arms wrapped round his torso. He loved that! Many were the saucy looks he gave me and sometimes I had to tell him to concentrate on his walking instead of grinning at me.

With this improvement Hap's attitude changed and he was nearly back to my old antagonist. He used to sit in a comfortable chair so he could see into the shop and call attention when someone came in: I teased him about being better than a bell.

For five years Hap continued a sort of half-life, but he was surrounded by and involved in his family. Inexplicably one day when I was away on holiday, he had another massive stroke.

His death left a hole in my life. I had loved the difficult old man: and I think he knew it.

A Typical Sark Cottage

6

As soon as Camp Farm became ours, Peter and I started to plan our new house. We both agreed that the old cottage was not salvageable so had to apply to the 'Natural Amenities' committee of the Chief Pleas. There were strict rules about housing development on the Island, but as this was a re-build we were not as restricted as people applying for a new house on undeveloped land. Legislation had been passed that only residents of ten years or more could build on new land: this was later amended to fifteen years. We were restricted to keeping the same basic outline and height of roof. This did not pose much of a problem as we did not want a huge place, although we would have liked to build high enough to take better advantage of the lovely view on all sides.

We chose a more substantial construction than the previous wooden building, and looked at various other places being built at the time. One that took our interest was by a Scandinavian firm. The floor was made of polystyrene blocks resting on a concrete base, and then topped with particle-board. It was ideal for our needs, as the concrete base that the old Camp Farm had been built on was not in good condition, and this would save having to break it up and start again.

I was a little sad to see the old building knocked down. It had been my home for all the years I ran the guest house, and although it was far from luxurious it had its memories. Before demolition I held a sale of everything we had left behind when we went to New Zealand. Peter and I were starting with a 'clean slate' and would have no use for the cutlery and crockery, beds, chairs and tables that had been left for our tenants. I could not stay to watch as the tractors and bicycles rolled up in the road bringing the keen and the curious to sift through the leavings of my former life.

Instead I walked up the road to one of my favourite areas: the 'Eperquerie.' The dusty road gave way to a double track with grass and weeds growing in the middle. On each side the stunted blackthorn bent away from the prevailing wind: mute testimony to the ferocity of winter weather. Now the verges were thick with autumn oxeye daisies and honeysuckle. Soon the path stopped in a deep depression where the horses and carriages paused to allow their passengers to marvel at the sweeping view. It never ceased to thrill me. The land dropped away sharply in swathes of brambles, gorse, bracken and ling heather to form a peninsula, narrowing to a distant point of rock and boulders. To both sides the brilliant blue sea stretched to the French coast on one side, and the neighbouring islands of Guernsey, Jethou and Herm on the other with Brechou nestling just off the Sark coast.

I took the path leading down to the left through hedges of ripening blackberries, soon coming to a viewpoint over Port Du Moulon and the aptly named gigantic natural rocks, 'Les Autelets.' They did indeed look like enormous alter stones, with seabirds wheeling about them and the sea churning at their base. Breathing deeply of the almond-scented gorse I continued along the path that took me down the peninsula and round the other side, tracing a route I had made many times before. I remembered my companions of previous walks: Hugo the Labrador, long dead, and my son Roy, thousands of miles away in New Zealand. But they were good memories and I made a resolution then, to stop looking back and enjoy my new life.

The sale went well and most items sold: those that did not I stored away for the next jumble sale. These Island occasions were an essential part of life on Sark. Not only did they raise an amazing amount of money for various charities, they became a social meeting place for friends and a fountain for information about what was happening on the Island. There were trestle tables loaded with mountains of good second-hand clothes. Some of the young people were expert at systematically working their way along the piles and extracting an armload. However it was unwise to put down your personal clothes anywhere near this table. I remember one old man, getting too hot in the packed hall and taking his outer garment off, yelling: 'Some bugger's just sold my coat!'

There were also tables groaning with home-made cakes, jams and bottle fruit: a children's toy stall and of course the 'tombola stall.' This was usually the 'piece du resistance' and had been the subject of much begging and cajoling for weeks. The organisers were seasoned jumble sale workers and well versed in this complicated art. The best contributions to the jumble sale were commandeered, along with bottles of wine, tickets for a meal, new toys and goods donated by the Island's shops. The night before, a display like a huge flight of wooden steps was set up in the hall on a table, with a sheet covering it. All the prizes were placed artistically on display, each with a raffle ticket attached with a '5' or '0' at the end of the number. The duplicates of these, along with many other numbered tickets were carefully folded and put in a bag. On the day of the sale, people were offered this bag to pick random tickets for a charge: this was normally priced at five tickets for a pound or 25 pence each. If you were lucky enough to get a ticket with a '5' or a '0' on it, then you won the appropriate item on the stand. Not all the prizes were attractive, but if there were some really good ones people often spent a small fortune trying to win: sometimes spending far more than the prize was worth.

Sark residents are the most generous towards charity donation that I have ever encountered. Maybe it is because there are no 'government handouts.' Everyone has to earn his or her income, but as there is no income tax the money in hand stays there. There are local taxes and duties, but it is seen where the money goes, and the Island does help those really in need. An example are the 'Professor Saint Medical and Dental Funds.'

A South African heart surgeon, Professor Saint, retired to Sark some years ago. One of his students, Dr Christian Barnard, was to be the first man to perform a heart transplant.

When the Professor died he left his considerable wealth to the Island in trust to help towards giving free dental care to the school children and to reduce medical costs for those in need. In particular, there was a supplement to the cost of medicines from the doctor, which he had to dispense as there was no chemist on Sark. Naturally this original trust diminished over the years and so the Island residents typically set about raising money to swell the funds. Many were the jumble sales, coffee mornings and more adventurous projects organised over the years to keep the fund solvent.

7

It did not take long to pull down the old building of Camp Farm, and once exposed the state of the woodwork became apparent.

'Just look at this,' Peter held up one of the roof supports, riddled with woodworm. 'I think we would have had this on our heads before long!'

As soon as the concrete base was cleared, we started to mark out where the rooms would go. We had already discussed plans with our builder, an experienced local man, so we had a good idea what we wanted.

The holiday season was nearly over, and people were not so busy looking after the visitors that swarmed to Sark in the summer. This was a cue for us to receive island residents who were curious to see what we were doing: and to offer advice. We took it all in good part, and as it turned out one comment proved to be invaluable.

'You want to make sure your corridors are wide enough for a wheelchair . . .you never know what is ahead!' I was glad at that time that I did not.

In the meantime, we had settled in the Old Farm. David slept in a room that he was modernising upstairs, with the only access up a ladder from the long kitchen. We had joint use of the kitchen and lounge and Peter and I had a bedroom upstairs and use of a bathroom. The trouble was that everything was being restored around us. All the ancient crumbling plaster was being stripped off to reveal the lovely granite walls underneath. This meant dust and rubble everywhere. There were few internal doors. A curtain over the gap in our bedroom afforded some privacy, although it did not cut out the autumn winds. The toilet flue exited through a large hole in the wall: at least there was no hanging about when you went in for necessary functions. After I packed the hole with old curtains it was a little more comfortable.

We were very grateful to David for the sanctuary while our home was re-built and helped as much as we could. Although at first David was determined to be independent and cook for himself, when the smells of the meal I was cooking for Peter and me wafted up to his room, it was sometimes too much for him. A head would appear at the top of the ladder: 'Er, what are you having for dinner? It smells delicious.'

I soon learned to cook for three (or four really as David had a good appetite) and a tactful 'I seem to have cooked a bit too much: would you like some?' sent David down with his plate to be heaped high. I thought it was the least I could do.

There was a 'Rayburn' stove in the kitchen, and I delighted in cooking on one again. I remembered with mixed feelings the 'monstrosity' that I had inherited when Ken and I first bought Camp Farm. The old solid fuel 'Rayburn' had caused me much frustration with its temperamental reaction to the wind direction. I did, however master it, and loved the food it produced, as did my many guests. As David's cooker was oil-fired it was far easier to control.

The days and weeks slipped by, and gradually my new life took its pattern. I had decided to use my returned airline ticket to bring Roy over for a visit in late autumn. As a special treat we also planned to take Roy to Switzerland for a couple of weeks. I had always fancied learning to ski and at the last minute my brother David who lived in Holland, decided to come with us.

'I'll teach you and Roy to ski!' A challenge that did not work for me as it turned out.

It was wonderful to see my son again. I had wondered if he would hold a grudge, but I did him a disservice. He was his usual loving self. Roy had known Peter when we had run our guest houses and they had always got on well, both having a similar sense of humour.

I had another reason for wanting to get Roy over to the Channel Isles. He was now in the top classes at school in

Auckland, New Zealand, and wanted to go to university to study computer sciences. The boys' school in Guernsey was particularly good, and I had been to see the headmaster to ask if a place could be found for my son, should he decide to finish his education in the United Kingdom. My brother had gone to Cambridge University and graduated brilliantly. While I did not think Roy was quite in his uncle's league, I knew he was very clever and I wanted the best for him.

'I'm sure you could pass the entrance exam for any of the UK universities. You could visit your father in the summer holidays, and maybe get a seasonal job.'

'It would be winter though, Mum. In any case, there is Annette, my girlfriend: and Dad.' I did not try and persuade Roy: the last thing I wanted to do was divide his loyalties, though I thought, wrongly that his affection for the girlfriend would not last.

'I suppose Ken would be lonely, especially as he said he'd never look at another woman.'

Roy looked a little embarrassed and blushed. 'Er, well, not exactly: you should see some of the women he brings home.' He quickly changed the subject.

We booked a hotel in Saas Fee, near Zermatt. It was a delightful picture-postcard village set in the Swiss Alps. We had all bought 'Moon Boots' and took all our warm clothing, which was needed as the snow was deep throughout the village and surrounding area. The ski lifts started right in the village, and it was not long before David took Roy off for his first lesson.

'You two would be best to try 'Langlauf,' cross-country skiing, it is a bit easier.' Easy or not I found I just could not stay upright. As soon as I got myself in the right position, with poles supporting me, my feet just slid forward and I landed on my behind each time.

'Huh: too much posterior ballast!' My brother was not much help at all.

Peter managed a little better and stayed upright, but never mastered the art of stopping, except by steering into the nearest snow drift. In the end we settled on long walks in the snow, exploring the local countryside. Roy did very well and seemed to be a 'natural,' much to David's satisfaction.

It was a good holiday and I was delighted to spend so much time with Roy. It seemed that he had not suffered greatly from his parents' separation: he was looking forward to his tertiary education and his own future. I was glad that Ken and I had waited until this time instead of when he was younger.

Chris in Switzerland

8

Roy's visit went too quickly, and I was very sad to wave him off at Heathrow Airport, but Peter and I had made plans to visit New Zealand before too long and had that to look forward to.

In the meantime there was great excitement on Sark. A film company had decided to record a series for television based on a book written by Mervyn Peake. This author and artist had lived on the Island in the 1950s. A group of like-minded friends had accompanied him, and they used a building called the 'Gallery' where they created and displayed their art. The building still stands to this day: now a well-equipped store and Post Office still keeping the original name.

The action of the book, 'Mr Pye' was supposed to take place on Sark and after the producer and director visited the Island, they announced that there was no better place for it to be filmed.

The story was a whimsical one, centred round the title's character, a rotund do-gooder. He decided that Sark residents should be encouraged to live perfect lives, directed by 'The Great Pal in the sky.' He came to the Island with that in mind and immediately recruited a lady assistant, a Miss Dredger. He had several meetings for all the residents, one of which was at a barbecue on one of Sark's stony beaches, Port du Moulin. Here he demonstrated that faith could overcome any obstacle, by hoisting an old lady, Miss George who was afraid of heights, up a high rock arch on the beach. He gave an impassioned speech standing on a rock, to the apparently gullible Islanders.

Mr Pye was so perfect that, to his horror, he started to grow Angel wings. The only way he could reduce these was to become very badly behaved: he then started to grow horns. For the whole of the four-part mini-series Mr

Pye performed a juggling act to balance the two unlikely attachments. It is assumed that this was a parody of man's fight between good and evil.

Eventually the residents became tired of this little man's activities and chased him all over the Island while he tried to escape, driving a horse and carriage. At the end he did escape by crossing 'La Coupee', the high natural causeway between Big and Little Sark, and flew off into the sunset. It was a highly unlikely story but the whole Island entered into the spirit of it, most signing up as 'extras.' To the delight of many of us the cast was world-famous. Mr Pye was played by Derek Jacobi, Miss Dredger by Judy Parfitt, and Miss George by Betty Marsden.

There were many stunts involved, in particular a final chase of the horse and carriage by most of the Island's population. This was where I came in. Some time before the arrival of the crew, the Doctor had asked if I would be available when dangerous stunts were performed, as there had to be a medical person on site and he was too busy. I had readily agreed especially as I was being paid but heard no more so assumed the company had made their own arrangements.

A few days after the filming started, I was helping David remove old plaster from the lounge walls: I was covered in dust from head to toe. The phone rang, and then Peter rushed in with a grin on his face.

'That was the filming company: they want you down at the harbour as soon as you can. They are doing a stunt and must have you there.'

I cleaned up as quickly as I could, grabbed my medical bag and hitched a lift on a tractor down the steep harbour hill to see an amazing sight. There was a mock-up of part of 'La Coupee', complete with railings constructed in the wide area where the tractors normally turned. There also was a black horse and a carriage, with a man standing in it with enormous realistic wings attached to his shoulders. Cameras and crew stood around, and a tractor and trailer with what looked like a pile of mattresses was drawn up close to the far end of the mock-up of 'La Coupee.'

A tall, slim man with a clipboard in his hands hurried over. He quickly introduced himself as the director.

'Good: thanks for coming at such short notice. We thought we had things covered but our medical adviser didn't arrive today.' He looked down at the clipboard. 'You won't have to do anything I hope, but the stunt man has to drive the horse and carriage over the. . . what do you call it?'

'La Coupee.'

'Yes, La Coupee: through the railings made of polystyrene and jump out of the carriage and onto the pile of mattresses.'

'Yes, right,' I said faintly, 'nothing to it.'

The stunt man set off and had a couple of trial runs.

'Right, now this time jump: O.K?'

The stunt man, who did look a little like Derek Jacobi from a distance, nodded and set off at a gallop. Half way across he leapt from the moving carriage towards the mattresses . . . and missed, landing heavily on the edge of the trailer and slipped to the ground. For a second we stood horrified, until I realised that I was needed. I rushed over to where the man sat on the ground rubbing his hip.

'Didn't allow for the bloody wings, did I?'

'Don't move for a moment: just want to make sure nothing is broken: you went with an almighty crash.' I felt carefully where he had hit himself and asked him to move his feet and legs. All seemed to be functioning well, but he looked pale and was shaking a little.

'You're in shock. I really think you should rest a little.'

The producer was standing by. 'O.K., Frank, you must go back to the Hotel. I think we got enough shots, anyway.' Turning to me he asked if I could go back with Frank and I agreed.

We got onto the back of the trailer, Frank lying on one of the mattresses and made our way up the Harbour Hill.

To my consternation he reached into a side pocket and produced a flask, taking a swig before I could stop him.

'What was that? You know alcohol is not a good idea after an accident!'

'I'll be O.K. It's not the first tumble I've had you know!'

When we got back to the hotel, I helped Frank to his room and he immediately started to strip off his clothes. It was not until afterwards that I realised I could have been in a delicate situation. At the time I concentrated on rubbing Arnica cream thickly on the rapidly darkening bruising on his muscular back and buttocks and getting some ice from the hotel bar for a pack.

'MM, that feels good, Nurse … I don't even know your name?'

'Chris.'

'Well, Chris, I want you around with all my stunts. You know what you are doing!'

It was a fascinating time for everyone involved. The filming crew stayed for a few months, and I had several more calls, but none as dramatic as that first one.

The cast and filming crew mixed with the residents: it was impossible not to on such a small Island. I was delighted on one occasion to chat with Derek Jacobi during the filming of the picnic on the beach of Port Du Moulon.

We were taking a break and I could not resist the temptation to talk to this actor whom I had admired for years. I had last seen him in a Shakespeare play at the theatre in Stratford-upon-Avon. I was nervous, but felt my uniform gave me some sort of official status.

'This is quite a departure for you, Mr Jacobi: I last saw you in 'The Taming of the Shrew' at Stratford.'

He gave his famous chuckle, and drawled, 'Weell, you know my dear, one has to try new things: don't want to get stagnant.'

'Ha, I can't see that ever happening.' I think I blushed: what a thing to say. I quickly changed the subject and we chatted about Sark. 'It is such a friendly place: and so beautiful. It is like a holiday to be here for this filming.'

I had to agree as I looked up at the towering cliffs, now topped with brilliant yellow gorse in flower. In every crack and ledge wildflowers bloomed. The sea was gently flowing in and out rattling the rounded stones as it moved, and gulls wheeled, crying overhead while the May sunshine poured down warming everything it touched.

'Yes and I am lucky enough to live here,' I said quietly as I got up to move away as filming started again.

For the weeks the filming crew were on Sark the weather stayed fine. The summer season had not started, and those visitors that were on the Island could offer to be 'extras'. Many did, and joined the queue at the makeup and clothing tables. Although most of the work was outside, lights and the bright sun made faces pale on film. Clothing and hair styles also had to be authentically 1950s, though as one wardrobe assistant quipped, 'Don't really need to change some of the residents' styles!'

Both David and Peter took part. On one occasion David was asked to go onto a beach when Mr Pye was trying to reduce his wings by being nasty to children playing together. He tried everything to make one little child cry, but as it was the son of one of the cast, the child just laughed when Derek Jacobi jumped on his sand-castle.

'Give the kid a pinch,' David was told. He hated to do it, but he was being paid. At the third try, the poor child burst into tears.

By far the most exciting event was the chase. This came at the end of the story but was filmed over several days and in different parts of the Island. The inaccurate sequence of locations caused much amusement for those residents who watched the final series on Television.

One very dramatic scene was not rehearsed and could have been unpleasant for one of the minor actors. He was leading a horse and carriage, planning to jump onto it and join the throng of people running up a steep lane. Suddenly the horse, frisky from a winter of inactivity, took off with the actor hanging on to the reins and running desperately by the side of the carriage. Fortunately the hill was steep enough to slow the runaway, allowing the driver to hop aboard.

'Brilliant!' exclaimed the camera man, 'We'll keep that in.'

On another occasion, as many Islanders as possible were asked to run as fast as they could along a road, waving their arms and shouting. The Doctor was free on that occasion and joined me out of sight behind a bank. 'Och, will you look at all my heart patients: I hope to goodness none of them have a coronary! I bet you my surgery will be full the morrow.'

The filming of the chase and other outdoor scenes would normally be by a camera mounted on a truck. As no cars were allowed on the Island the camera crew had a problem. A horse and carriage or tractor would jolt too much. The situation was solved by a 'Deux Chevaux' car being shipped over from Guernsey: the soft suspension was ideal, and with the engine disconnected and towed by a horse, a compromise was reached.

The old and the new 'Camp Farm'

9

The rebuilding of Camp Farm had progressed while I had been preoccupied with the filming, and we decided to move in before it was properly finished. We were going to do the decorating ourselves, so decided to finish the bedroom suite before we moved in. This consisted of a luxurious bathroom, large bedroom and dressing room with a full length built-in wardrobe.

The new Camp Farm looked very different from the building we had pulled down. Instead of wooden walls, they were solid concrete made to look like granite painted over, with the corner coins of granite showing: it had proved too expensive to have all granite. The walls must have looked realistic as one local man remarked; 'What a shame to paint over that stone-work!'

The roof was in Spanish-style pantiles. This was not common on the Island and drew a few comments until the bright orange colour mellowed.

We decided on double glazed UPVC window frames with inset battens to give the effect of smaller panes. This proved a mistake over the years as the plastic yellowed in the strong sunlight.

The front door was custom made in hardwood, as was the big five-bar gate by the road and a smaller one giving access to the front garden.

The old building had four bedrooms, a lounge, kitchen, back lean-to storeroom and a sun-lounge. The new one had less, but larger rooms. Besides the main bedroom en-suite, there was a large kitchen with walk-in pantry, office-cum spare room and a big lounge/dining room. We added a separate laundry and entrance reception area with toilet and cloakroom. The wooden chalet that Ken, Roy and I had slept in while running the guest house had a small bathroom and kitchen added. It was to prove very popular with the stream of friends and relatives who visited us in the years to come.

The lounge was beautiful. Remembering the main room of a beach house Ken and I had built in New Zealand, I suggested taking the roof up to the rafters and having exposed beams. The builder thought it a good idea.

'I'll have to box in the three supporting girders, but I can make them look like solid beams. I suggest you stain them before we get them up, though. It will be much easier.'

We did that, but unfortunately one of the workmen brought his dog on site, and it got into the lounge while the stain was still wet. It was not until the beams were in place that we noticed faint dog foot-prints across one of them. It made a good conversation piece when we held dinner parties later as we never painted them out.

Some time later, we discovered one disadvantage with the hollow beams. Peter and I were sitting in the lounge after dinner one evening when I thought I heard a pattering and squeaking overhead. We had had a rat and mouse problem in the loft in the rest of the house, but as there was nothing but the roof above, we could not decide where it was coming from: then we realised the animals were having fun running up and down inside the boxed beams.

The rest of the roof-space was for storage and to accommodate one of Peter's hobbies: a model railway. We installed a strong folding ladder and as soon as he could, he started to plan a layout. It was to occupy him for many hours and I helped with the scenery.

When we were planning the house, we decided we must have an area for dinner guests to change and freshen up. As there are no cars on the Island, walking and cycling are the general means of transport. So if you are invited out to dinner on a wet and windy night, there is no point in a wearing good shoes or a woman wearing makeup. It was and still is the practice to don waterproof footwear, waterproof coat and usually leggings as well. Arriving at the host's house the visitors strip off wet gear and shoes and spend some time getting into party clothes. We planned an entrance hall with adjoining cloakroom, large mirror, toilet and washbasin: essential if you did not want mud and rain walked through the house.

When Camp Farm was a guest house, Ken and I had used the two and a half acres that were part of the freehold to run a smallholding. Our three goats and donkey grazed the good grass, and the four 'fold units' that housed our 200 chickens were moved frequently, so we needed every part of the land. When Peter and I moved in, we realised we only needed the large front lawn and enough at the back for a sizable vegetable garden.

We offered the rest to David, who was only too pleased to use it. He eventually pulled down the old corrugated iron shed that had been built in the far corner of our fields, and built a wooden barn which was a vast improvement.

The garden was a challenge. The front lawn was just rough field grass with a few trees Ken and I had planted, closed in by banks and a privet hedge along the drive. Eventually we planted fruit trees at one side, and shrubs to the other, making a 'wild' garden with rough grass and a path. The centre was cut finely to give a smooth lawn. There had been a gate through the front bank and Veronica hedge leading onto the road, but we closed that in, preferring access at the side. This gate was made locally and the carpenter also dug the holes for the posts: then left everything in true Island tradition, for several days. Fearing that someone might fall in the hole, I went out the morning after they had been dug to put a piece of wood over. Looking in I saw what looked like a child's ball, and realised it was a small hedgehog rolled up: it would have been unable to climb out.

I rushed back into the house and grabbed a pair of kitchen gloves. Gently I lifted the little animal out, and it uncurled in my hand. I looked with horror at its eyes: they were covered in blowfly eggs so I called to Peter; 'Can you hold this little fellow and I'll wash his eyes.' We managed to remove all the eggs, as I knew they would hatch and the maggots would eat their way into the hedgehog's brain.

Within a few days the little fellow, which I named 'Prinny' from a child's story, recovered: but what to do with it? We had seen an adult hedgehog scuttling past the side of the house for several mornings. 'Maybe that is the mother,' Peter remarked, so we placed Prinny in the path that we had seen the other hedgehog take. Early that morning we were awoken by the most unearthly screaming, like a child in pain. We rushed out to see the adult attacking Prinny: the poor little thing had no defence, and although Peter pushed the larger animal away with a stick, the baby died soon afterwards. It was a sad lesson not to interfere with nature.

The hedgehogs were a sign that winter was well on the way. Although the climate in the Channel Islands was mild by comparison with most of the United Kingdom, they headed for hibernation.

With our recent experience in mind, Peter and I made a special note to search for other wildlife in the large pile of wood and branches that was accumulating in or adjoining field.

November 5th was approaching, and thinking it was a good way to dispose of piles of wood from the old building, we had rashly offered an Island Guy Fawkes party at Camp Farm.

Despite the fact that my kitchen still had no cupboards, just a free-standing oven unit, hob, fridge, sink and planks supported on trestles, I was hosting a group of helpers and catering for an un-known number of revellers.

One lady made a huge vat of pumpkin soup, another brought rolls, while most of the men brought beer. We started potatoes baking in the oven, then transferred them, wrapped in foil, to the edge of the fire. Sausages arrived, already cooked and a worker at one of the Island stores brought fairy lights. It reminded me so much of New

Zealand, where everyone 'mucked in:' suddenly we had a great party on the go. A couple of the men collected all the fireworks and organised their firing, for which I was relieved: the last thing I wanted was as accident. I discovered later that the men were volunteer firemen and had even thought to notify Guernsey about the bonfire party.

It was a wonderful evening, and helped to establish me on Sark. It became an annual event for a few years until David needed the land, and then someone decided it would be a good revenue for one of the local charities, and charged for the food. Somehow it lost something.

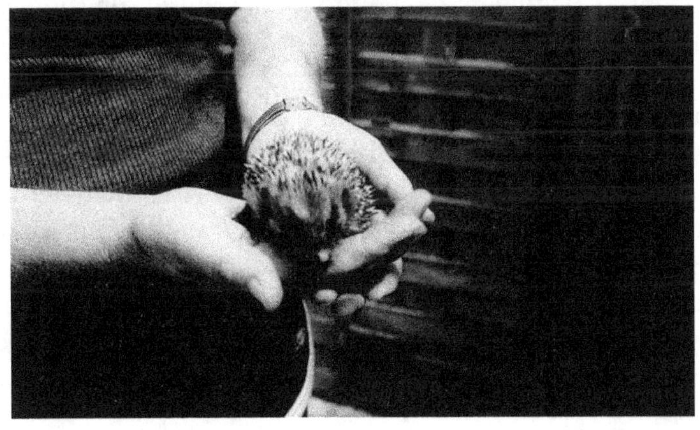

The hedgehog 'Prinny'

10

Peter had been singing in choirs for many years. He had a fine baritone/base voice and I loved to hear him in the church choir, and one day he asked me if I would like to join.

'I can't read music. I was in a choir in our London church years ago when Ken and I were running a youth club but it was mainly to keep the peace, as there was a bit of friction.'

'Go on: I'm sure the choirmaster will tutor you.' The Vicar was choirmaster and an inspiration to all would-be singers. He took me on with two other hopefuls for extra practice, in his study. I am sure some of the noises we made at first would have made Mozart turn in his grave. However at last it made sense and I was able to hit the notes, even if I did not know which ones they were! I bought a 'Beginners Guide to reading music' and joined the Church choir. It was one of the best things I had done since I arrived back on Sark. I made friends that would last for many years and began an interest that I have enjoyed for the rest of my life.

For a population of only 500, St Peters church had an amazing choir of around 25. We often sang in four parts, rendering responses and an anthem most Sundays. The choir was in demand to sing at weddings and funerals. It was a commitment as we were expected to attend rehearsals every Thursday and the service on Sunday morning.

As Peter and I were not married we both had qualms about going to church and went to see the vicar soon after I returned to Sark.

'Would you marry if you could?'

'Of course.'

'Then I feel in the eyes of God you are.' It was a comforting advice, but my upbringing still made me a little uneasy and we neither took communion for some time. It was a personal decision we made, until one Easter when we were in Gloucester Cathedral on a visit to Peter's daughters. When the call to go forward to the alter came, we looked at each other and knew it was the right time.

I loved the Gloucester area. I had my memories of working in Cheltenham. Before that, my home in Stratford-on-Avon and nurses' training hospitals in Birmingham had been near, and I had explored the lovely Cotswold villages on holiday. I was delighted to have reason to visit again and soon after my return to Sark Peter and I began a long association with the 'Three Choirs' Festival.'

One day soon after we had moved into our renovated Camp Farm a large package arrived in the post. It was full of glossy leaflets showing the glorious Gloucester Cathedral on the front.

'How would you like to go to the 'Three Choirs' next year? It's in Gloucester.'

'I don't know anything about it. Is it listening to three different choirs all the time? Not sure I've the stamina for that!'

Peter laughed and showed me the timetable.' It's called the 'Three Choirs' because one year it is in Hereford the next in Worcester and the next in Gloucester and the choirs of each cathedral play significant parts, but it's a varied programme.' He opened one of the brochures.

'There are some choral pieces: especially early and church music but there are also orchestral concerts, talks, special banquets and readings.'

I spread the brochures out and spent a while studying them. My introduction to classical music had been by Ken and his choices were heavy going at times. He was well into plainsong and church music. Peter was too, but leavened it with less heavy stuff like Simon and Garfunkel and The Seekers. We both loved medieval pieces as well as music from the Lloyd Webber musicals.

As Peter had said, I saw a variety in the Three Choirs Itinerary. It was a whole week of orchestral concerts, talks, banquets, performances in the Cathedral as well as in smaller surrounding churches and Prinknash Abbey.

'We can't possibly go to them all, so we need to decide which we prefer. Oh look. . .Brian Kay is giving a talk: we must go to that!' Peter was really excited. He had known the Kings' Singers since they used to visit Sark some time before they formed their unique group. When he ran his guest house and tea garden they had enjoyed his famous cream teas. I even remembered taking Roy in his pram on one occasion to meet them.

Brian was the bass/baritone singer and had the most wonderfully rich voice I had ever heard. It had a liquid, warm sound with the feeling of a smile not far under the surface. I could listen to his speaking voice too. for as long as he cared to talk. We both agreed we could not miss that.

For the next few days we pored over the brochures, finally deciding and booking our choices. We were fortunate that Peter's daughter Lyn and family lived not far from the centre of Gloucester. It would have been impossible to stay in the city otherwise as accommodation prices increased and everywhere became full to capacity.

For many years this became a fixed date for us every third year when it was in Gloucester. Eventually we became ushers, which was great fun. Our duties were not onerous, and I delighted in our need to wear evening dress on most occasions. Peter looked resplendent in grey waistcoat and tails, and I bought several re-cycled evening dresses and skirts. We were invited to a few special functions including the Lord Mayor's banquet.

I remember one in particular, during a very rainy summer. As we were about to leave the Town Hall, the heavens opened. Nothing daunted, Peter and I donned our Sark wet weather gear, consisting of heavy waterproof jacket and leggings. I still remember with a chuckle the expressions of the other ushers as they watched me tuck Peter's coat-tails down his leggings before I bundled my long skirt into mine.

One other benefit that grew from our attendance at the Festival was a chance for Peter to meet the performers. He was always on the lookout for artists who would be willing to visit the Channel Islands during the summer, and give concerts.

For some time Peter had been involved with the 'Channel Islands' Music Council.' Members from Guernsey, Sark, Jersey and Alderney engaged professional performers to visit the Islands, and Sark was fortunate to benefit. Many of the artists were top performers and if the larger Islands had not subsidised the smaller ones we would not have been able to afford them.

As it was we had a double pleasure, as some of the artists stayed overnight with Island residents, and we had our fair share at Camp Farm. Our little chalet was very popular as it gave a degree of independence. We supplied meals, which sometimes were at odd times. Performers usually liked a light meal before a concert, but afterwards, with adrenaline flowing, they needed another substantial feed. I remember once half-jokingly offering a big 'fry-up' at midnight. . . and was accepted.

At other times a trip to the Pub was needed and of course we trotted along. Once we accompanied Nigel Kennedy whom we were delighted to have on the Island, for a drink and I spent the rest of the evening worrying about the multi-thousand-pound violin tucked on the bench-seat beside me. On that occasion he was staying at one of the hotels. It was situated deep in valley and there were no street lights, so we escorted him. . .and the violin, I with my heart in my mouth. I never did get my torch back.

Some performers became good friends. Alan Schiller, the delightful pianist, first stayed with us while performing and then returned for one or two short holidays with us. Once he came with his two young sons and another time with his new second wife. There is a story he tells against himself that happened on that visit. Among the visitors' attractions is a prison building, said to be one of the smallest in the world. Keen to show off his local knowledge, this proud new husband said; 'Well of course it is not used these days.'

A face appeared at the barred window and yelled; 'Yes it bloody well is!'

I have other memories of this pleasant man: his requesting a publicity photo of himself, getting on a bicycle dressed in evening dress and tuxedo and his fascination with a newly-hatched chick that I had put under my desk light to dry-out. I remember those gifted hands cupped round the yellow and brown fluffy mite: and the occasion when he was introducing a concert in our village hall, a cat wandered up the aisle and sat looking at him. Without missing a beat he said something like; 'Well, that wouldn't happen in the Wigmore Hall!'

After all these years we still write occasionally and have met several times since.

**Peter and Chris dressed up for the Three Choirs
Festival**

<h1 style="text-align:center">11</h1>

Soon after joining the church choir, I was chatting to a Sarkee friend as we robed for the Sunday service. She mentioned that she had just been for a swim in a hotel pool and then had breakfast at the hotel with a group of friends.

'We call ourselves 'The Sark Dippers and Plodders'. We swim in the summer and sometimes walk in the winter.' I asked if I could join, and after a short waiting list I was delighted to be included.

The hotel where we met, Petit Champ was to my mind one of the best. It was run by a delightful couple, Janey and Terry Scott and later by Chris and Caroline Robins who became firm friends of Peter and me. It had been a traditional farmhouse, and over the years had been added to, becoming a luxurious hotel with some of the best views on the island and a superb restaurant.

The swimming pool, set a little away from the hotel, was in the quarry that had been made when the farmhouse was being built. It was secluded and surrounded by bushes, and theoretically heated by solar panels. In reality the water was extremely cold at eight in the morning, when we all met to swim. It was the practice to begin our weekly swims about Easter and end when the hotel closed, usually early October.

With the sun not yet over the surrounding bushes changing was done quickly. Most of us arrived by bike already in swimming costume and outer clothes, and after the swim changed into a dry costume. It was so much easier than struggling with underclothes on a damp freezing skin.

My aim was to do up to 30 lengths, but usually started the season by four very quick widths in water temperature of around 54 degrees Fahrenheit. Shivering but with a tingling skin and a justifiable smugness we walked up the steps from the pool to the covered conservatory at the front of the hotel. Here we soon warmed ourselves round the heaters and gratefully accepted the offered large glass of ginger wine that soon became a tradition.

We were usually ushered into the dining room before most of the guests left their rooms, there to order and consume fruit and cereal, followed by a huge fried breakfast: we felt we had earned it.

After the experiences of trying to change under a towel held by numb fingers, I hit on the idea of my 'Sark Beach Buddy.' I bought a piece of towelling or two beach towels and made a changing robe. I had seen those from years ago, like a small tent with an elasticised head-hole, but mine could be worn as well as used for changing. I stitched a seam at the shoulders and down the sides, leaving a large gap at the top for the head and at each side for the arms. It had to be wide enough to get your arms inside to remove clothing. I finished it with a tie belt. The hotel sold several and they were popular with the Dippers and Plodders and Island visitors. My sales slogan told it all 'You can change under it, wear it and dry on it. What is it? It is a Sark Beach Buddy!'

They were not the only things I made. I had always been keen on dressmaking. As a child I used to make my dolls' dresses and costumes for one of my hobbies, marionettes. When Ken and I moved to Sark to run our guest house we had little money to spare. I made most of my dresses and some of Roy's clothes when he was little. There was no need now to do that, but I still enjoyed sewing. I learned that there was a sewing group attached to St Peter's Anglican Church. I approached one of the organisers, but was surprised at her reaction.

'Oh I don't know, Chris: you know Marjorie comes and it might cause some friction.'

I was about to insist that we were good friends, but I knew the power of the gossip on the Island, so I called to see Marjorie. Peter and I were in the process of decorating the outside of her cottage and we sometimes had a chat. I told her about what was said and so we devised a plan.

Next sewing day we marched in arm in arm: we were delighted to see the jaws drop. From then on we both attended regularly.

I had never tried embroidery but was keen to learn. I started with a couple of cross-stitch cushions which I still am proud to possess. Most of the work was in order to build up stock for sale at the annual Church Fete and there were some beautiful items. Some of the ladies were expert knitters, while others produced children's clothing, embroidered gift cards, tablecloths, aprons, peg-bags and even dolls. One year I made a male and female doll, dressing them in the traditional Guernsey Victorian clothes. Many years later the little female doll came back to me, bought by a friend in a jumble sale. I have kept her too.

It was a novelty for me to be able to join in the many activities on Sark. When I had lived there before, between running the guest house and smallholding and nursing, I had no spare time.

I became involved with the Church fete and freely offered my services: so much so that there was a rather caustic comment from one lady; 'I guess you will be running it too, soon.' I realised I had to be careful not to tread on toes; I was still on probation.

One job I enjoyed for several years was to supervise the children's fancy dress which started the 'Fete'. I was dressed in the traditional long skirt, blouse, apron and Island bonnet. These were much prized on the Island and often had been handed down for generations and impossible to buy. I was fortunate to be lent one by my friends Annie and May.

I would meet all the hopefuls outside the church at the set time and parade them down the Avenue, the Sark main street, with a child holding a placard advertising the Fete. I soon learned that it was necessary to have an adult or responsible older child at the back to hurry on the stragglers.

We made our way to the top of the Harbour Hill in time to meet the tractor-drawn covered seating transport, which locals called 'The Toast-rack'. This was a novel way of getting passengers to and from the Guernsey boat up the steep and winding hill. We were there to meet a group of Guernsey Traditional dancers, who were also going to judge the fancy dress. This done, we all returned to the Vicarage lawn where the Fete was held. With fanfares and music the event was opened by the vicar. My duties done, I then usually found myself in charge of one of the stalls. After a while, the Guernsey dancers, all in wonderful period dress, performed a series of traditional Channel Island dances.

There were cream teas available as well as a cake stall; plants and farm produce; bric-a-brac; apple bobbing; books for sale; throw the hoop; and of course several tombola stalls. In later years I found myself in charge of the bottle stall. This was a major fundraiser and often brought in several hundred pounds. Work for this needed to start several weeks ahead. I made posters and leaflets and distributed them all over the Island as well as to all the hotels and licensed premises. A day or two beforehand I phoned around the pubs and hotels as a reminder and to arrange pickup or delivery. I expect I was a bit of a nuisance but everyone took it in good part. As one person said, 'Well, it's my way of giving to charity.' In many cases people delivered but sometimes I needed to collect: it was a busy time for me as I had to cycle all over the Island.

On the day I had to get to the Vicarage early to set up my trestle tables, cover them with the provided sheets and erect the overhead banner announcing the stall and charges. Previously I had arranged for several helpers to come along. It was a very popular stall and usually needed at least three, sometimes four people behind the barrier. Some bottles would have arrived and others were delivered as the morning progressed. Anything was welcome, from wine, water, shampoo and always some crowd-drawers of spirits and liqueurs. Often I had two or three hundred bottles, as the hotels and pubs were particularly generous, sending a whole crate of wine.

The job then was to stick a number, usually ending with a '5' or '0', on each bottle. The duplicates of these were then folded and put into two clean plastic buckets I had brought. To these were added many folded non-prizewinning tickets, and they were well mixed.

People were offered tickets from the bucket at a usual charge of 25 pence a ticket or five for a pound. If they got a ticket with a '5' or'0' there should be a prize on the table. There was always the nightmare that one of us may have given the wrong prize previously in a rush, and the number was no longer there. I learned to keep a few spare bottles of wine behind in case. Another lesson I learned was to keep one or two attractive prizes to one side until half-way through the afternoon. A large bottle of whiskey or gin would attract customers and if it went too early, the attendance tended to drop off. It was then time to produce the 'extra.'

At the end of the day all the clearing up began. The boys in the back room, Peter among them, counted up the money and we then had a tot of something stronger than tea to celebrate.

It was not quite over for me. I had a lot of 'thank-you' phone calls to deliver. After all I had to think of the next year.

12

When I had lived on Sark with Ken, we had been in the habit of attending the Methodist chapel when we could. A group had formed that I had become involved in, to invite speakers, have religious discussions and offer a cup of tea and refreshment afterwards in the Methodist chapel hall. While I had been away, this had grown and moved to the cafe at the side of the Island hall. It had ceased to have religious overtones and gradually a lunch club was created. On my return to Sark I became very much involved with this and we introduced a talk or short film afterwards. As we met on a Thursday, we called ourselves 'The Thursday Club.' There was no membership fee and anyone could attend, but primarily we wanted to encourage older people living on their own to come and socialise. It became the highlight for some and proved very popular. The set roast meal was cooked by the people who lived in the accommodation at the hall and who looked after it. The standard was excellent and the cost reasonable.

We tried to get interesting people to talk in the meeting after the meal. Sometimes it was a visitor to the Island: sometimes a resident who had done exciting things, and sometimes a home movie of holidays. For a while these meetings were well attended, but gradually less and less people stayed after the meal and in the end after several years, it just became a lunch club. The Thursday Club continued to meet when a new Island hall was eventually built, and has become a social get-together for a larger number of Islanders: a far cry from the original group that began many years ago.

Such socialising was new to me. When I had been living with my parents, and later as a student nurse, I seldom ate in a restaurant. For one thing I could not have afforded it, and it was not the accepted practice in those days. Later, with my husband Ken it was not something we did, either, except while on the ships on our way out to New Zealand.

'Too expensive: anyway why eat out when you are such a good cook?' Ken was not one for squandering money.

Peter's background had been different. As a University graduate and then an executive employee in England, he had become used to dining out. I had to learn how to cope the hard way, but I learned quickly.

My first lesson was when we went away to the Lake District for a few days soon after I had left New Zealand. Peter took me to a top-quality 'dining experience': one of the best restaurants in the country.

I had no idea how to order and was overwhelmed by the opulence and decor. There were at least six courses, each leading into the other, with wines to match. My big mistake was to order lobster bisque as an entrée. By the time I reached the third course I was full and could only mumble my apologies to the head waiter who asked if there was 'anything wrong with madam's meal?'

Before I returned to Sark, I had learned how to order meals and even used my cook's intuition to diagnose those dishes we most enjoyed. I had always loved cooking, which was just as well, for eventually Peter and I hosted many dinner parties and regularly went to one or other of the excellent restaurants that had opened on Sark.

We made friends with several couples who liked to dine well and developed the habit of dining at each other's houses. My menus from guest house days were not sophisticated enough, but I learned to adapt and studied my cookery books. I had to learn about a starter other than soup. One that I invented has stood me in good stead throughout the years and was quite simple and very popular. First, peel a large orange or pink grapefruit and segment it, keeping any juice. Mix about one teaspoon each per person of natural yogurt and mayonnaise in a bowl and add a small amount of the juice, a little honey and some mild curry powder. Lastly quarter a peeled and de-stoned avocado, liberally sprinkling with lemon juice to stop it going brown. On a small plate spread a little of the mayonnaise mixture, fan the avocado on one side and the segments of orange or grapefruit on the other and garnish with a sprig of mint.

The main meal was always a challenge. A roast was acceptable, but I wanted something different sometimes. So I boned a leg of lamb and stuffed it with rosemary and apple. Chicken was also popular, and I discovered a great 'lemon chicken' Greek recipe, using chopped herbs and brandy. This could be served with new or sauté potatoes and green vegetables. I became keen on Chinese cookery too, after I bought a 'Ken Hom' cookery book. When Peter and I occasionally visited London I liked to visit Soho to get ingredients, especially the fermented soy beans that were essential in one of my favourites: 'chicken in black bean sauce.'

When it was time to produce the desert, it was usual to present two: one a light fruity one and the other more substantial. Some of my guest house favourites came in here: lemon butter tart; lemon surprise pudding and chocolate fluffy pudding, (see *'So you want to Live on Sark'*). I also adapted one which used our home-grown bottled gooseberries. After the fruit was drained, and placed in a deep dish, corn-flour and soft brown sugar and some water was added to the juice and heated to thicken. After cooling, 3 to 4 separated egg yolks were mixed in to make a thick custard and folded into the gooseberries, keeping them whole. A meringue was made from the egg whites and placed on top and cooked till the meringue set. This could be served hot or cold.

Another favourite that I borrowed from a hotel in Jersey we sometimes visited, was oranges in Grand Marnier.

With Peter's work and his involvement with the Channel Islands' Music Council we frequently had to entertain at home, or visited the other Islands for meetings. The Music Council met every few weeks in

Jersey and Guernsey but once a year visited Sark and Alderney.

When there was a meeting in Jersey in September or October, most years we had a few days holiday in a delightful small hotel in St Brelade's Bay. The restaurant had won some acclaim and we thoroughly enjoyed our visits.

We also visited the other small Island of Alderney, and had a week or so holidaying there. We made many friends through the Music Council on this delightful Island. It is about the same size as Sark, but the population is three times more. There are cars and tar-seal roads and the beaches are much more accessible, but it is still a beautiful place to visit. There was a friendly rivalry between the two smaller Islands, and we described Alderney as 'fifteen hundred alcoholics clinging to a rock.' It was true that there were a few heavy drinkers in both Islands.

I remember once being told a story that the entire front row of a concert held in the afternoon in Alderney fell asleep after a heavily liquid lunch. The concert was stopped and the artist dryly remarked that if he could stay awake, please could the audience do likewise.

As the Island of Alderney was quite a distance from the other Channel Islands, the normal transport was by small airplanes. These three-propeller planes took few passengers and there was no aisle: each couple of seats folded back as people were seated in order, and then the seat was put back for the next couple. There was only one pilot, but if the plane was full, sometimes a passenger sat next to the pilot.

There was a story of one loaded plane waiting for the pilot, and a man in a heavy coat got into this seat. As everyone sat waiting for the pilot, this passenger started fiddling with the controls. Turning round he asked, 'Anyone know how to fly this thing. . .I've always wanted to have a go!' and slid over to the pilot's seat. By this time the passengers were becoming alarmed: until he took off his coat, revealing a pilot's uniform underneath. The date was April 1st.

The 'Boys' School

13

Another big change in my life was the chance to go away on holiday with Peter. I had always had a yen to travel since an early age. The three trips to New Zealand by ship had whetted my appetite, as had the two years travelling around New Zealand. Now we both were financially able to plan exotic trips, particularly in the winter.

'I want to see Roy as often as possible.' After our wonderful holiday in Switzerland, I was desperate not to lose touch with my son.

'Yes, well we should be able to go every three years or so and Roy can come over in between.'

So with that agreed, we looked at other places nearer home. We settled on Scotland for our first big break.

'I have a standing invitation from one of my clients.' Peter mentioned a well-known Scottish family with Royal connections. 'We could go and stay the weekend, then go by train up to the Kyle of Lochalsh and over to Skye:' he thought a while, then said; 'Maybe by train right up to Inverness.'

It turned out to be a memorable trip. I shall never forget the first weekend. By this time I had acquired a little poise but staying in a minor stately home put me to severe test. Our host and hostess were typical of those born to a privileged lifestyle. Realising I was a little out of my depth, they tried to put me at my ease.

'We won't dress for dinner, if you prefer?'

'Oh', I blurted out, 'I have a special dress for the occasion!'

'Then of course we will, my dear.'

Which was a mistake: my yellow silk was no match for the sleek 'designer labels.' However nothing was said, of course. The dinner was served by servants in kilts and the table glowed with crystal and silver. It was all the glossy magazines and films portrayed, and while a little nervous at first I was able to relax and enjoy my first, and I suspected my last, experience of: 'How the other half lived.'

At breakfast the many dishes on the sideboard were covered with silver lids and I recognised Spode china on the table. I shamelessly ate all I was offered, and particularly enjoyed my first taste of smoked salmon and scrambled egg. In the afternoon we took the dogs for a walk over part of the estate. Here I held my own by encouraging my hostess to discuss her husband's medical problems, while the men strode ahead. People are always happy to talk over health issues and I think I redeemed myself a little.

Although I had enjoyed myself I was relieved when we were driven to the station in a Rolls Royce to catch the train. We were both delighted that some of the way was by steam. Peter was a fanatic about anything to do with railways, and I had become interested too.

The place we stayed in Skye had a tennis court and we were piped in to dinner by the son of the owner: it was a lovely place to stay. We hired a car and toured the island: 'We must come back one day.' We agreed: but we never did. There were so many other places to visit.

Our next big holiday was to New Zealand.

'What say we stop a few days in Singapore?' It was my first time there and I fell in love with the bustling vibrant and totally safe city. At that time Singapore Airways were offering very cheap overnight stays in top quality hotels. We spent three nights in the Hilton: a place we could not have afforded otherwise. There was a good Chinese restaurant within the complex, so we decided to treat ourselves.

'I never can get used to these blessed things,' muttered Peter, waving his chopsticks over his bowl. Without a word, one of the beautifully dressed waitresses approached with a rubber band. She retrieved the chopsticks, applied the rubber band and handed them back to Peter with a sweet smile. Problem solved.

We just had to visit Raffles. It still showed the 'colonial' décor, but was soon to be renovated. I felt, in subsequent visits, that it had lost some of its charm and was glad I had seen it on that first visit.

I refused the mandatory 'Singapore Sling' as I hated gin, but we both decided to see the floor show on offer. A man with a huge python appeared on the stage and asked for people from the audience to come and have it draped over their shoulders. I looked round, but everyone was studiously looking at the floor. I do not know what made me do it. . . I hate snakes . . . but I found myself up there with it writhing round my neck. To my surprise it felt warm: I had expected it to be cold and slimy. When I exclaimed to the man on the stage, he just shrugged and said: 'Well what do you expect, with the temperature at 40 degrees?'

It was wonderful to see Roy again, and Ken had found a new wife. Mary was well known to me as she had been Roy's leader in Scouts. Her second husband used to look after the engine of my Hospital Board car when I had been a district nurse in New Zealand. Roy was at University by this time, and he and his school sweetheart were living together in a house Ken had bought as an investment. We stayed a little time with them, and it was good to get to know the girl who would soon be my daughter-in-law. They were both well-suited, and 25 years later they are still together.

When Roy decided to go to university, I had bought him a car. The only stipulation was that I could use it when I visited New Zealand. So transport was not a problem.

Peter and I planned to tour around and first spent some time with the relatives he had discovered several years ago. Their ancestors had settled in Hawke Bay on huge tracts of uncultivated land. It was wonderful to get to know this typical hard-working farming family. Their farmhouse was built of Kauri, with the traditional veranda around and polished Rimu floors. I was proud to be accepted readily: sadly they had lost a daughter of about my age, who also had been a nurse, and I felt I was a temporary substitute.

I have memories of the old farmer calling his cows in to be given hay feeds: of being driven over endless steep hills and meadows in a rattling old Land-rover with no doors, clinging desperately to the window frame to stop myself falling out, and of a traditional barbecue that took hours to prepare from logs which first had to be burned down for charcoal.

We spent some time exploring by car, staying in motels most of the time. It was a far cry from the time when Ken, Roy and I toured in a Bedford delivery van, but the magic of this lovely country was still there.

If I had been living anywhere other than Sark, I would have been sad to leave New Zealand, but the lovely, tiny Island still had its pull.

It was a long trip back home, and the most frustrating was usually the last leg, from London to Guernsey and then to Sark. It was impossible to expect to do it in a day. We often had to stay a night or so in London and one in Guernsey too, as so often the Sark boat times did not coincide with the flight times. We were very fortunate to have two wonderful friends, John and Jill living in Guernsey, and their beautiful old farmhouse was almost a second home. Sometimes we arrived when they were out; collected the key and took their dog for a walk.

We would always study the weather forecast on those occasions with some anxiety. Strong North-Easterly winds and a low tide would mean no boat from Guernsey to Sark could run, as they could not tie up in the usual Maseline Harbour, and the older Creux harbour would be dry.

However an exciting holiday we had had, it was wonderful to see the white lighthouse hanging precariously from the distinctive cliffs heralding our return. Our pace of life slowed as we told our carter what luggage to collect from the boat, knowing it would eventually find its way to our door. We would sometimes walk up the steep harbour hill or get a ride up, walking the rest of the way home. We would be bound to meet people we knew who would greet us and ask after the holiday. It was at times like this you did not mind everyone knowing your business.

Back home, the kettle on and a cup of tea on the way, we would drop in a chair and say; 'It is so nice to be home.' Then a few weeks later Peter would be planning the next holiday.

14

The year after our trip to New Zealand, the whole Island was in a state of excitement and anticipation. Queen Elizabeth was due to visit Sark to open the new Medical Centre.

Previously the doctor had lived in an old house on the Island, with the waiting room attached. It had very thick walls and the way from waiting room to the doctor's surgery was through a narrow stone corridor set in the wall. I had often wondered how a very fat person would manage as it was so narrow. The consulting room and dispensary were inconvenient. The doctor had to supply as well as prescribes medicines, as there was no dispensing chemist on Sark, and he needed an up-to-date storage facility.

The new centre and accommodation is luxurious in comparison. There is a large conservatory at the front, leading into the waiting room, with a patients' toilet. For the doctor there are a surgical room, consulting room, dispensary and a secretary's room. The accommodation is spacious, with several bedrooms and bathrooms and a lovely area for a garden. It was well built and a plaque had been set into one wall, as commemoration. It was this that the Queen was to unveil.

A Royal visit to Sark was, by most standards, low key. In an Island where crime was practically non-existent and people rarely locked their doors there was little fear of terrorism. However the usual security precautions had to be taken, and day-visitors were restricted. We residents had the unique chance to be very close to the Royal visitors, and I even had a chat with Prince Phillip.

As a nurse I was needed to stand outside the Island hall in case anyone was taken ill, while their Majesties were greeting the local dignitaries inside. Two people were required, so I asked the help of a very attractive young nurse who had come to live on Sark with her family. We were standing to attention in our uniforms by the door when the Queen left the hall, followed a little while afterward by Prince Phillip. Catching sight of my attractive helper, the Prince stopped.

'Oh, I didn't know there were nurses! Are you always here?'

'Well, no sir,' I stammered misunderstanding the comment. 'We don't stay by the hall all the time; we visit homes around the Island.'

'Hm! The Doctor said nothing about you. He must be keeping you to himself, lucky fellow!'

With that the Prince strode to the waiting carriage.

Over the years Sark has been a popular place for Royalty to visit. Its peace and beauty are an attraction, but in addition it has an independent relationship with the Crown, dating back centuries. The Seigneur is directly responsible to the Queen, not the British government.

Prince Charles in particular, indicated his delight in the uniqueness of Sark when he visited a few years after the opening of the medical centre. This visit was to commemorate the 50th anniversary of the liberation of the Channel Islands from German occupation during World War 2.

For most of the war the Channel Islands had suffered under German occupation, and Sark residents had had a tough time, although some of the occupying force were not hostile in their treatment of the Islanders. One such German had been studying medicine in his home land when he was called to serve his country. He became a medical orderly and eventually found himself on this tiny Island.

Here he met and fell in love with a local girl. After the war he returned and married his sweetheart and has stayed on Sark ever since. He helped to bring up his family, opened his own business and acted for many years as a volunteer ambulance attendant and first-aider.

For his service to his own country, this gentle man was awarded a decoration by Germany: and for his service to

Sark he was also awarded a decoration by his adopted country: a unique situation.

A reception was held in the old Island Hall for Prince Charles to present the medal: this time I was fortunate to be invited to the reception. I particularly remember Prince Charles putting aside his prepared speech and saying how wonderful the Island was and declaring: 'Don't let anyone force a change on you.' This sentiment has been very hard to support over the years as outsiders time and again have tried, and are still trying to change the constitution and the beauty of the natural cliffs and fields.

One unfortunate incident occurred a few years before Prince Charles' visit. For some reason a young French unemployed nuclear physicist decided that Sark should be returned to France. Several centuries ago the Channel Islands had been part of the Duchy of Normandy, until Queen Elizabeth 1st of England granted the first Seigneur, Helier de Carteret, the right to occupy Sark with 40 landowners or 'Tenants'.

This misguided Frenchman posted notices around the Island saying that he was going to take over occupancy at noon. He then sat on a bench outside St Peter's church dressed in battle fatigues and with a loaded rifle. Just before the appointed time, the Constable and his assistant approached this Frenchman and while one spoke to him, the other managed to disarm him from behind. It was a very brave act.

Sark does not have a traditional police force: annually a local man or woman is elected by the Island as 'Vingtenier' or junior constable to assist the Constable who normally would be the previous year's Vingtenier. They received some training, but mainly came from the fishing and farming community.

During Royal visits police and security men are brought to the Island and inspect all the areas to be visited. On one occasion two men crawled underneath the Old Island hall to look for explosive devices: they found none, but it is reported that one remarked that he did not know what was holding up the floor.

Whether this was the final deciding factor or not, soon afterwards the plans for a new school and hall took fruition. Much discussion for and against combining a new school and community centre followed, but eventually plans were agreed upon and an attractive new building was erected.

Prior to this the infants were housed in an old building called the 'Girls' School' near the prison and the older children in the 'Boys' School,' near the church and Old Hall. Neither building was modern, with the children's toilet separate, and becoming cramped with the increasing young population. While the hall had done great service in years gone by it was decided that a new place was needed to act as a centre where a good meal, a drink or two and socialisation could occur. The design was Scandinavian, with a lovely high-ceilinged main hall: a pub-like bar upstairs: a well-run cafe/restaurant downstairs and several smaller rooms for meetings.

There was some dissention about having the combined school attached in the same building, as some thought having licensed premises so close would affect the youngsters. In fact it does not seem to have caused any problems as the school day is finished by the time serious drinking takes place.

It was an inspiration and has proved to be a focal point for Island activities, with a large playing fiend adjacent.

**The visit of Queen Elizabeth and Prince Phillip
with me on duty outside the Island Hall**

15

Nursing Hap was my new beginning to nursing on Sark. After seven years as sole district nurse in a rural New Zealand area, I had learned a great deal. For most of my remaining time on the Island I was privileged to work with the doctor. I attended many residents, both Sarkee and English and seriously thought of starting a district nursing service, and approached the medical committee with that in mind. I particularly wanted to train a few local girls in 'nurse-aiding' and was keen to have a 'woman's clinic' as the doctor at that time was not comfortable with female problems.

However, soon after I returned to Sark, the 'old' doctor retired and the new one was trained in obstetrics, as well as being experienced in minor surgery, so the committee decided to leave things as they were.

I was a little disappointed but was soon involved with as much nursing as I wanted. In previous years, the retiring doctor stayed on the Island, and so if he was needed for a short 'locum' while the new doctor had to go to Guernsey, he could stand in. However new laws had been introduced regarding a doctor's insurance, stating that he must pay for a whole year, just to do a few days' work and so the retiring doctor decided not to re-insure.

Soon after his arrival, the new doctor asked me to call in to his surgery. We had already met and I liked him very much.

'Chris, I am in a bit of a spot. I need to go to the dentist next week and wondered if you could stand in for me?' I had already been in touch with the Royal College of Nursing, who were responsible for my insurance cover, regarding responsibilities outside a nurse's normal experience.

The reply stated: 'As long as you do not diagnose or prescribe, and you have contact with a qualified doctor, we do not see a problem.' So I was able to say that I was happy to help out. This was to be a 'baptism of fire.'

Although it was not the busiest holiday season there were several day-visitors on the Island. As there are no cars on Sark, many people delighted in hiring bicycles and exploring the lanes and footpaths. Some of these paths were not suitable for cycling, particularly when ridden by inexperienced people. My first casualty was one such ill-advised lady who did just that, falling heavily on her shoulder and knee on a steep footpath.

The system for dealing with casualties was well organised. If a patient needed to go to the hospital in Guernsey, the St John there had a very fast ambulance launch called 'The Flying Christine.' The medical person in charge in Sark phoned the St John headquarters: explained the circumstances and was told the expected time that the ambulance launch would arrive at the Sark Harbour. The Sark volunteer ambulance men were then alerted to collect the patient in the tractor-drawn ambulance and to arrive at the harbour to meet the launch.

In this, and in subsequent occasions, the Headquarters had been alerted by our doctor that I was locum. A doctors' surgery in Guernsey had also been informed that I was on call, and I could contact them for advice if necessary: this was the days before mobile phones. In later years it was much easier and I could contact our doctor directly.

As soon as I was alerted about this accident, I rushed to the site, taking my, and the doctor's medical bag. I also took a blanket as I suspected some major problem as the patient was said to be screaming with pain and unable to move.

I had taken several advanced first aid certificates, and it did not take long to realise the lady had broken her collar bone and dislocated her knee. I gave what first aid I could and sent someone to phone our ambulance. When they arrived I ran home as it was not far away, and phoned the St John. Within an hour of my seeing her, the unfortunate lady was in the Guernsey Hospital.

I was amused, when I reported to the doctor on his return, to hear his story. The dentist's surgery had a wonderful view from above the harbour and over to Sark and Herm. He happened to glance out of the window from the dentist's chair and was horrified to see the ambulance launch making for Sark.

For the many years this excellent and versatile doctor practiced on Sark, I was privileged to work closely with him on a private basis. I also took patients not referred by him, but always discussed the treatment. I stood locum on many occasions, and had some unusual experiences, but none as bizarre as once when I was on call overnight.

It was the doctor's practice to leave a note on his surgery door when he was away, with my phone number. On this day the current constable phoned me in some agitation.

'Old Fred was out with one of the drivers and has collapsed: Chris can you come and see him?'

'Where is he?'

'We drove to the surgery; realised you were on call and unharnessed the horse: he's still on the carriage.'

I knew the old Sarkee well, as he was one of the Island's characters. Too old and frail to drive by himself now, his wife used to let him go out with a younger driver, theoretically 'instructing' the young woman, although she was fully qualified. Thus they preserved his dignity and could keep an eye on him.

I did not like the look of the old man as soon as I clambered onto the carriage. The absence of a pulse confirmed my suspicion. 'I think he's dead,' I whispered to the constable, not wanting to alarm the inevitable bystanders.

'So do I', the constable whispered back.

'I think we had better harness up the horse and take him home. Can someone quickly go and warn his wife, please?'

As we approached the old farmhouse, the man's wife rushed out. 'Are you sure he's dead. Sorry, but you are only a nurse. I must have a doctor! Someone go and get the retired doctor. You must try to revive him!'

Protest as I might she insisted the patient was carried into their bedroom and nothing would satisfy her but that I give mouth to mouth resuscitation. I shall never forget the sensation of the cold lips on mine and the breath I blew in, nauseatingly seeping out as I bent to give another breath.

Fortunately the retired doctor, who apparently was a personal friend, arrived soon and confirmed my diagnosis.

Other incidents caused some amusement. There was the time the wife of a local dignitary phoned and asked for help in having a bath.

'Chris, I've cracked my ribs and am having difficulty, could you pop round, do you think?'

I agreed, and asked what had happened.

'Don't laugh: I fell in a grave!' I tried not to laugh and went to help the unfortunate lady.

I got the story as we sat having a cup of tea after I had helped with the bath.

'Well, I was standing at the dug grave to drop in a flower.' She took a sip of tea and winced as she moved to set the cup down; 'you know our old gardener died? Thought he'd like that: I turned round to follow everyone who'd already gone into the church and slipped on the wet grass.' She picked up her cup and took another swallow and gave a grimace; 'Before I knew what had happened I found myself at the bottom of the grave on my back.'

'How on earth did you get out? They could have lowered the coffin on top of you.'

'Exactly my thoughts: well I yelled blue murder and fortunately I had been missed and they came and hauled me out. Felt such a fool!'

Her husband had just come into the room. With a grin he sat down opposite his wife.

'Bet it's the first time any of your patients came out of the grave, Chris.'

The 'Ugly Sisters' from Sark Theatre group's 'Cinderella'

16

Although there were only 500 residents on the tiny Island there were many talented people living there. It was common to find that the man decorating your house had been an actor or producer, or that the carriage driver had a university degree. People went to Sark for the unique life there. Peter used to say; 'You can do two things regarding your work; decide to do a certain type of work and go where it takes you, or live where you want to, and do whatever you can find there.' Many did the latter on Sark.

This may have been the reason that an excellent theatre group developed. One resident had been involved with theatre, and was an artist; I believe he had also been a lighthouse keeper in his time. It was not long after I arrived that I became involved with the theatre group as wardrobe mistress. It was discovered I liked dress-making, and I allowed myself to be persuaded to take the position that no-one else wanted. I soon found out why. The ex-producer was a talented director, but suffered fools not at all and demanded a degree of perfection that was difficult for amateurs. This extended to the costumes, and we had many an argument during the several years I battled with him. We eventually formed a good working relationship, although on one occasion, when he demanded six new costumes a week before a production, I was near to quitting.

I did enjoy the challenge and had great fun at the jumble sales grabbing anything that might come in useful. Everyone entered into the spirit and I often came away with my bike piled high, to wobble to the home of a kind resident who let us store everything in his loft.

I would never have managed if I had not had a wonderful backup team to help. Each production had to be organised from the beginning. From the first rehearsals I used to attend to take measurements, jot down notes and then spend some time with the producer who would have his own ideas. Sometimes I would have to modify his outlandish proposals, but it was a matter of pride to try and accommodate him. I do not think I let him down, and some were certainly a challenge. I remember one production about toys, and I had to make several soldiers' costumes, complete with red jackets and shiny high black helmets. Cardboard covered with black rubbish bags worked well. The jackets were recycled several times in later years, with some adaptation.

Two productions I remember especially. One was a lavish version of 'Cinderella' for which I needed to make 70 costumes. Of course I did not make them all, but spent much time and enjoyment in making the garish ball costumes for the ugly sisters and stepmother. They were played in true pantomime tradition by men. It was strange that while they went about their work as farmers or carters the young men were quiet and unprepossessing. But put them in drag costume and greasepaint they became flamboyant, hilarious music-hall characters. One scene that merited the standing ovation it received was performed at a scene change. The lights were dimmed and a blue spotlight shone on the stage. To the music of Swan Lake four rather large ballet dancers dressed in white tutus that were picked up by the lights, gave a fair performance. It was only when the house lights came up, that the audience realised the dancers were four young men; one was David. I had not told Peter and I thought he was going to fall off his chair with laughter.

The other memorable production ran for the whole of the summer season. Normally the plays were performed on a few days only.

One of the five hotels on Sark was in a deep valley, and had lawns around it with mature trees at the edge. It was an ideal location for Shakespeare's 'A Midsummer Night's Dream.' We were fortunate that the weather was fine for most of the time. It was a challenge for the actors as they all had summer jobs, and they had to juggle their lives to fit in weekly performances. The costumes were not too difficult, but I was proud of the one I made for 'Puck.' There was a weeping copper beech at the edge of the performing area, and I contrived to stitch some sprayed artificial ivy leaves to match. These I sewed onto a flesh-coloured body suit. The actor was excellent, and stood so still within the overhanging beech leaves that he seemed to appear from nowhere. An artist on the Island made the donkey head: that was beyond my ability.

The lawn of the hotel sloped like a natural amphitheatre and gave seating for the audience while the actors performed in and out of the surrounding trees. It was truly magical to see the daylight fade as the last songbirds went to bed and the spotlights came on. I felt Shakespeare would have been quite at home as the actors played their parts.

One of the actresses had become an important part of David's life.

When David was renovating the Old Farmhouse he had decided to divide it into a couple of units. When we left, he told us that a young woman was taking one of them. To Peter's obvious interest he hastened to add;

'She's just a friend: nothing else. Hilary drove a carriage last year and has returned a second season to Sark to work and needs somewhere to stay.'

When we met this lovely young woman we both had our fingers and toes crossed, but were sad when her boyfriend visited for a weekend.

'Looks as if she's spoken for,' muttered Peter. He had taken an instant liking to this bright young woman; she was not only beautiful, but intelligent and strong.

'As a trained Norland Nanny, she'd make a wonderful mother, and be able to help David with his farming.'

'For goodness' sake, Peter: don't you go saying anything!'

Peter had been right. A few weeks after the boyfriend had gone home, David and Hilly came round to see us.

We were sitting in the garden having a cup of coffee when we saw them walking hand-in-hand over the lawn.

'Look at that: told you so,' Peter muttered.

We chatted for a while, and wondered why they kept lifting up their hands: until I saw a flash of light on Hilly's left hand. 'Oh: Oh. Is that what I think it is?'

It was; we brought out some bubbly and celebrated what has turned out to be an enduring and lasting relationship and marriage. Hilly has supported, worked with and encouraged David and produced two delightful children. Peter could not have wished for a better wife for his son while the grandchildren, Pippa and Charlie have been a delight to both of us.

I have had the joy of being an honorary 'Auntie Chris' for many years, and Pippa's mercurial temperament often made me feel she could have been my blood granddaughter.

Pippa and Charlie

17

It was not long before David and Hilly announced their wedding plans: as it turned out it was to be in the same year that my son and Annette decided to marry in New Zealand. That was quite a year.

In October we all went over to UK to Hilary's home in East Anglia. Here we met her family and had a wonderful stay.

Hilary looked stunning as a bride, being driven up to the ancient church in her father's prize Alvis car. David naturally turned up on a tractor.

We had decided to have a boat holiday on the Norfolk Broads while we were near. So, soon after the wedding, we travelled the short distance to this interesting area criss-crossed with canals and waterways. Neither of us had much experience with boating, but thought a small motor boat would be easy to manage. How wrong can you be?

One of the problems was that it had been a very wet year and all the rivers and canals were higher than normal. Many of the bollards used to tie up the boats were under water, and difficult to locate. Peter took charge of propelling the boat which was to be our home for a week. I was delighted with the interior, like a small caravan with minute kitchen, a pull-down bed and a tiny bathroom area.

'Look Peter, if you have an upset tum, you can use the facilities, be sick and have a shower all at the same time!'

After a while we developed a routine: most of the evenings we could berth at one of the quays and delighted in eating at a local pub. Peter became quite expert at backing into a small mooring space. Sometimes we had to tie up at the side of the river and I had one close call when Peter almost pulled me into the water. I jumped ashore, wading up to my ankles and scrabbling around in the water to find the bollards. I tied the forward rope and waded to get hold of the stern one. Peter gunned the engine, but instead of pulling into the shore, he shot outwards: if I had not let go of the rope I would have had a ducking.

Another time I performed an action that I would have found impossible if I had time to think about it. At the bows we had a small mirror, rather like a car's wing mirrors, to enable the person steering to see behind. It protruded quite a way above the bows, and normally would not have been a problem when we went under a bridge. With the unusually high-water level there were some that left no room. Usually we folded the mirror down in anticipation. On one occasion we had forgotten to do this, and I suddenly realised we were heading straight for one of these low bridges. There was a narrow ledge at either side of the cabin, scarcely wide enough for one of my feet. I managed to sprint along this ledge and with a rugby tackle pulled the mirror down just as we slid under the bridge to a cheer from people standing up above.

Despite these few occasions and indifferent weather, we thoroughly enjoyed ourselves. The area of Norfolk on the eastern side of England had a rare beauty of its own. Flat for the most part, you could see for miles across waving rushes and golden grass. Occasional windmills, reminiscent of Holland, stood majestically throughout the area. Some were still in working order, while others made unusual homes for the adventurous.

As always it was a pleasure to return to Sark, but we had little time to relax, as in December of the same year we travelled out to New Zealand again for Roy and Annette's wedding.

It was all a little bizarre. Ken had remarried and his mother had left London and moved in with Ken and Mary in a flat under their house. I think she never quite forgave me for 'abandoning' my family, but she was settled in her adopted country, and glad to be with her only child. It could not have been easy for a woman of 80 to leave the city of London where she had lived all her life and move to a rural location on the other side of the world. Whatever she felt about me, she kept to herself and I tried to be on my best behaviour. I had a genuine affection for her, but had never been able to penetrate the staunch Methodist reserve.

Soon after our arrival we went to visit Ken, Mary and Elsie.

'Be careful, Chris,' Ken warned me, 'Bitza lives with Mother now and he's got very unfriendly with strangers; he's going a bit blind.'

I nearly remarked that I was hardly a stranger to my little dog. Bitza had been mine until I left New Zealand, and it had been hard to abandon him. As that had been five years ago I did secretly wonder if he would remember me.

As I walked into Elsie's flat, the little dog rushed over to me barking and with his hackles up. He skidded to a halt as he almost collided with my leg: stopped short mid bark and sniffed me, and suddenly started to wag his whole body whining with joy. I could hardly believe he had remembered me after all that time. It was a happy reunion but I had a stab of conscience, thinking again how I had disrupted so many lives.

'You only have one life, Chrissie, and everyone seems settled and happy now...even little Bitza as Elsie needs his company.' Peter was a consolation, and it was true that Ken and Mary were happy together; Roy and Annette were getting married and Elsie content to be with her only son.

We were staying with Roy and Annette who rented one of Ken's houses. With Elsie's contribution he had been able to buy a couple of houses to let; something I knew he always wanted to do.

I still found it strange that young people nearly always lived together for a while before marrying, and that the bride usually wore the virginal white when she was anything but. However I had to admit that it was quite a good idea to discover if you could tolerate your partner's personal habits before total commitment.

I was glad of the chance to get to know my future daughter-in-law and managed to break down the initial natural antipathy she had for me. Having spent too much time in hospital with complications of her spina bifida, she disliked nurses. Coupled with that Elsie's comments about a mother who had abandoned her only child, had not endeared me to the young woman. I made the mistake, when I first met Annette, of giving her a big hug. As she had not been brought up with physical shows of affection, I felt Annette shrink from me. 'Oops,' I thought, 'wrong move!' In later years we made a joke of; 'I'm coming for a hug,' and 'Oh let's get it over with then,' compromise.

The four of us lived for a while together in the house before the young ones married. I was delighted to see more of Roy, and gradually Annette and I got used to each other. Peter and Annette never did get to like each other unfortunately. I think Peter's very English sense of humour annoyed the young woman: he could be a little 'over the top' sometimes. Peter never really understood what it must be like to be highly intelligent woman, but to be treated as mentally slow, just because she was in a wheelchair.

Roy and Annette were to be married in a picturesque church not far away, and Mary, Annette's mother and I went over the day before to decorate it, and meet the vicar. While we were chatting, I was amazed to notice that the vicar had a car key with the emblem and name of Sark embossed.

'Goodness, how on earth did you come by that?' I explained that I lived on the Island.

'What a coincidence. It belonged to my daughter and she gave it to me.' He lifted it up for me to examine, and continued, 'When we lived in Hamilton, she had several pen-pals. The one in Sark was a young woman called Belle.'

'Goodness, I know her. She's the daughter of a friend of mine: what a small world!'

This happy occasion set the mood for the second delightful wedding of the year. Everything went well and Annette's parents, Ken and Mary, Peter and I and Elsie shared a table at the reception.

I had become increasingly uncomfortable however during the two weddings and visits on holiday, to being called 'Mrs Curtis' and having to correct people. I decided that I would investigate the possibility of changing my name by deed-poll.

It proved quite simple: after the necessary forms had been completed I had to visit my solicitor. Here I had to swear that I no longer wished to be known as 'Mrs Davies' and henceforth was to hold the title of 'Mrs Curtis.' I did choose to keep the 'Davies' as part of my Christian name, as it was my son's name. It was a sad occasion in some ways: Peter was not with me and it was almost like a wedding without the groom.

The weddings of David and Hilly and Roy and Annette

18

One person that was not able to travel all the way to New Zealand for the wedding was my mother. My father had died the previous year after many years of suffering with Parkinson's disease. Peter and I had unfortunately been away on holiday during the short critical time of his sudden attack of pneumonia and death. My brother David had not been able to contact us until too late, and all the arrangements fell on his shoulders.

As soon as I could, I drove up to Bridlington in Yorkshire where my parents had moved. My mother had been born in the seaside resort and her family lived there so she had support during the long years of my father's illness.

I always thought of Phyllis as my mother, but she was my stepmother. We were very close and I loved her dearly, so I was devastated to see how suddenly she had aged in the few months since I had last visited. Her life had been totally devoted to care of my father, and now her 'raison d'être' had gone.

'Oh Chrissie,' she sobbed as I held her close, 'make the most of your life with Peter. You never know what is ahead.' Those prophetic words delved deep into my mind and I had a sudden panic at the thought of life without 'the love of my life.' I wondered how it was possible to survive when the other half of your existence disappeared.

We tried to get Phyl to move to Sark: I even had plans drawn up to convert the spare room to a bedsit, but in the end she preferred to remain in the lovely bungalow she had shared with my father. She did come over for several holidays and I remember one amusing incident when I took her to a Thursday Club lunch.

My mother had been a great beauty in her day, and still showed it. Among the people sitting round the table was a notorious gossip well known for being outspoken. She looked at Phyl and remarked; 'She's very beautiful your mother, isn't she Chris?'

'Yes, well, actually she's my stepmother.'

'Oh well, that accounts for it then: you aren't much alike are you?' My laughter was a little forced.

For several years Phyl insisted on staying on at her bungalow. I visited as often as I could, and she became more animated when I was there. We used to take trips out onto the Yorkshire moors, often taking her older sister Ethel with us.

There came a time when she was just not coping at home. We tried 'meals-on-wheels' which she declined to eat: I had another go at persuading the stubborn old lady to move to Sark.

'I don't want to leave Bridlington where your father is buried. Maybe I'll look at a nursing home.'

We spent several of my visits driving around and visiting places. Eventually she agreed to try one in the centre of the town, not far from her sister's house.

I was unhappy as I left the frail old lady, so different from the mother I had admired and loved most of my life. As I looked back and waved, I had a feeling that I would not see her again.

Just a week after I returned to Sark, the phone rang just as we were going out for lunch. It was the Matron of the nursing home.

'Oh, Mrs Curtis: something dreadful has happened. Your mother slipped in the hall and fell. She has broken her hip and is in Bridlington hospital. It wasn't our fault: I hope you...'

'Are they going to operate?'

'Yes, tomorrow.'

With a sinking feeling I remembered the many patients I had nursed while matron of a small medical and post-operation hospital in Auckland. So many had died from delayed shock, about ten days after such a trauma.

The fall happened on a Friday, and Peter suggested I wait over the weekend, but my feeling of premonition persisted and I took the first flight from Guernsey that I could. I picked up my car from Lyn and managed to get to Bridlington by Sunday.

When I arrived at the hospital I was concerned to see my poor mother sitting, dressed, in the day-room.

She burst into tears when she saw me: 'Oh Chrissie it is so painful. I just want to go to bed.'

'And so you shall, my dear.'

I knew it was medically correct to get patients up soon after an operation, to avoid the possibility of a thrombosis, but my heart was leading my head where my dear mother was concerned.

I stormed into the nurses' office. 'My poor mother is in agony. Please put her back to bed: I will take all responsibility.'

Eventually they did as I asked, and Phyl was happy to sleep most of the next few days. I could see she was failing, and the end came quite dramatically.

I spent all day at the bedside, and on the final day, just as they were serving supper, she suddenly said;

'Chrissie, Chrissie, I need the commode quickly, quickly!'

I rang the bell, and amid grumbling, two nurses lifted Phyl onto the commode, returning a little later to lift her back to bed.

I looked at her white face as they put her back, and I could see she was dying. I said nothing and just held her hand and stroked her forehead till she slipped away.

Then I rang the bell again. Amid more grumbles the two nurses returned.

'My mother has just died.' As they started to ring the bell and fuss, I added; 'please don't resuscitate: she wanted to join my father.'

For all my brave words: I had a good cry in the carpark.

One consolation for Phyl had been our two cats. Peter was an absolute 'cataholic.' He could not think of a life without one in his home and I loved them too. Soon after we moved into Camp Farm we decided to investigate the more unusual cat breeds.

'But not Siamese.' I told Peter about a little Siamese I had when I was a district nurse in New Zealand. She had been appropriately called 'Prima Donna' as she completely ruled the household.

After weeks of searching the newspapers, we discovered there was a breeder of British Blue and Silver Spotted cats in the nearby Island of Jersey. We read about these unusual breeds and liked the comment that they were intelligent, affectionate and full of character. We phoned the cattery and booked two kittens. Expecting to be away for several holidays we agreed that two would be company for each other. David and Hilly said they would look in to feed them and they could live in the laundry where we had put a cat-flap into the door.

All we needed was the two kittens: we had to wait several months as one of the breeding cats was producing a genetic fault. At last we had the awaited call from the owner of the cattery. She was a very large lady and had a wheezy voice which always made me smile: it sounded so much like one of her cats; 'Mhelowww; I've got a little felhoww for you; from a litter of crossed Blue hwith spotted. You have waited so long I'll let you have hisss sister though she would be perfect for breehding.'

So 'Mungojerry' and 'Rumpleteaser': 'Teaser' and 'Jerry' for short, came to take over our lives. As kittens and young cats they lived up to their names taken from T S Elliott's poems about cats. If there was a crash in the lounge, and the lamp was on the floor. . .no cats were around: if the lower decorations on the Christmas tree were scattered all over the house: no cats were responsible: and if a half-eaten rabbit was jammed in the cat-flap, it got there by itself.

The article was right: Jerry and Teaser were certainly full or character. They were beautifully marked grey tabby with distinctive spots. Teaser was silver-grey and looked like a small Ocelot, a type of African wild cat. She had a temperament to match as she was very much 'her own cat:' offering her affection on her own terms and with her own restrictions. Jerry was much darker in colour but had a loving temperament and was never happier than when he was draped over Peter's shoulders. I never got used to his suddenly springing from the back of a chair onto my shoulder: he was a heavy animal and nearly knocked me over.

Despite their long pedigree our cats were excellent hunters. It was an ideal life for them with freedom to roam the surrounding fields and no fear of being run over by a car in the road.

Teaser's speciality was rats. She used to spring from behind and bite the back of the neck of an animal often bigger than herself, hanging on until it sank to the ground dead. Jerry's was rabbits. Sometimes I saw the two working together as Teaser herded a rabbit towards a bush where Jerry was crouched, waiting to spring out and deal the death bite, or sometimes to play with it first.

They were not always good friends when they grew up. Often Teaser would spit at Jerry as he walked past for no apparent reason. He would put up with this for a while, then suddenly spin round and soundly box his sister's ears. They were certainly entertaining and we grew very fond of them for the many years they lived with us.

Jerry finally died of cat Aids. The vet was not sure how he got it, but he lived until he was 14 or so. Teaser was nearly 19 when her kidneys stopped working.

'Jerry' and 'Teaser'

19

The residents of Sark have always been adventurous. Put it down to the environment where they habitually face situations that would make city-dwellers quake, or just a need to be different. Whatever the reason, the re-introduction of the 'Sark Water Carnival' became a challenge that few of the most adventurous could resist. The carnival had been active in the past and I do not know why it was discontinued, but soon after I arrived back on Sark it became an annual extravaganza that drew the crowds.

The main features were the entries for the 'Flying Machines.' These varied from realistic-looking mini-planes and rockets, to people dressed in any type of costume, not necessarily, but sometimes, related to flight. The idea was to launch from the quay in the old 'Creux' harbour during a high tide and try to fly, before plunging into the water below. Very rarely did anyone take flight, but the descent into the water was pure entertainment.

Each year there were weird and wonderful machines produced, with smoke billowing from the rear: fireworks crackling and loud noises exploding deafeningly to cheers from the attendant public. There was, unfortunately a dangerous element, and some participants were hurt as the appliances became tangled with their makers.

Money raised was for the Professor Saint Medical Fund, and so the doctor was in attendance. He usually arrived by decorated boat to open the Carnival, and occasionally had to give his professional services too.

There were many other activities for people to enjoy: raft and swimming races: a greasy pole extended over the water that the young men could try to scale, and a special lobster and champagne lunch for those wealthy enough to enjoy it.

This luxurious meal was organised by one of the hotel owners, and took place on an arm of the old harbour that could only be reached from the sea. Diners were ferried over by dingy to climb up a metal ladder and those watching were given some entertainment. I remember one older lady who had obviously spent some time preparing herself with liquid refreshment. Try as she might she could not co-ordinate her legs into having both either on the ladder or in the dingy. Eventually a strong fisherman placed his shoulder under her ample posterior and virtually carried her up in a fireman's lift, to a cheer from the onlookers. I did not see how they got her down afterwards.

For some years on the 10th of May, Sark held a cavalcade to commemorate the liberation of the Island from the German occupation. On the 50th anniversary there was a particularly extensive one and I decided to enter too with a decorated bicycle. I wracked my brains, until Peter casually said with a grin; 'Have you ever noticed that you and the ambulance launch have the same name?'

So I entered as 'Flying Christine 1V', with a big placard and my uniform. I won a prize; though I am not sure I deserved it as I needed to do little preparation!

Many of the floats were works of art, and the use of tractors and horses added to the attraction.

These activities were appreciated by visitors as well as residents, but there were one or two shows that were more for those living and working on the Island. One of these, which has sadly disappeared due to the reduction in numbers of dairy farms, was the cattle show. At the time I returned to Sark there were several farmers who supplied milk and butter on a regular basis from their herds of Guernsey cows. The quality was superb: the milk was rich with a buttercup-yellow cream that churned into special butter that was much sought-after although I have to admit I was not very keen on the strong flavour.

Each year the farmers competed in a traditional show that could have come out of a Thomas Hardy novel. For days before, records of yield were kept, cow's coats groomed and udders cleaned. On the day, cows, calves and occasionally a bull were taken along to a specified field where a marquee had been erected. In this pats of butter with fancy patterns embossed: jugs of milk, curds, and sometimes cheeses were displayed.

In a roped-off area in the field the cows and calves were paraded in a sedate procession, to be viewed by intense white-coated judges gripping clipboards. The only excitement would be when the bulls were displayed, as they were hard to handle.

The horse show, is far more lively, and is traditionally still held in a tree-shaded field next to the Seigneurie. There are many lovely carriages and horses on Sark, though not as many as there used to be. Some of the older 'Victorias', a low-slung carriage with hoods, have gone. Many of the carriages used now to take visitors around are large wagonettes that can seat more passengers. They do not have the elegance of the older vehicles.

The horse show gives the public a chance to see the few older well-preserved carriages left: those that are used when there are Royal visitors to the Island. These carriages are paraded and judged by specialists brought in, often from Jersey. After the carriage display, the fun starts. In an island that still relies on horse transport to some degree, there are some wonderful animals used on a daily basis. There are classes for appearance, behaviour, horsemanship and later on, fun races. Occasionally Sark has had a rare treat when its own Champion Gold Medallist Karl Hester has visited the Island of his birth and demonstrated his superb dressage skills.

Although some visitors will call in to the horse show, it is an Island occasion. As soon as you have paid your entrance fee, you can wander around looking for your particular friends who will be sitting next to the roped-off arena. You make a detour to the tea tent to get a cup of tea and piece of delicious home-made cake and then sit down on the grass to catch up with the latest Island news. You lie back and look at the leaves waving under the

blue, blue sky, and wait for the next class to be judged:
there is no hurry.

A Sark Tea Garden

20

The 'Sheep Race Event' is quite a different story. Peter was involved in organising the very first one on Sark in 1997, and for several years used his considerable organising ability to make this a success. I think it appealed to his quirky sense of humour and I was happy to help: it was good to be doing things together. It has proved a popular and enjoyable outing for residents and visitors alike, drawing many day-trippers to the Island.

It works like this: for some weeks a local sheep farmer accustoms six or seven of his more docile ewes to being handled and to respond to his sheep-dog. On the day, they are taken to a field which has been prepared the night before. A long 'race-track' is cordoned off and stalls and marquees erected which offer items for sale, food, and games of skill. In one location an area is allocated for the 'Ascot' crowd who arrive decked in fancy hats and waistcoats, which will be judged later. There is also a betting tent.

While people arrive and place their bets which are controlled to fifty pence each, the sheep are readied for the first race. A small stuffed 'Jockey' usually in the shape of a rabbit or monkey with a racing hat and jacket, each a different colour, is carefully tied on the back of a sheep. When all is ready the sheep are released from the holding pen at one end of the course and the sheepdog herds them to the other end. The one that first reaches the marker at the end is the winner and those that bet on its colour collect their winnings. That is the theory.

The problem is that often the sheep do not want to be herded, or to run. I remember once they all turned round and stared at the dog and refused to move. On another occasion it was decided to put some bales of hay for them to jump: a sort of steeple-race (called 'sheeple-race' on the programme.) The contestants stopped and grazed on the obstacle, so it did not work very well.

I offered to man a stall during the first 'Sheep Race Event' but took a little time to wander around first, as I knew there would be little time once everything began.

It was a strange misty early morning, and it all added to the atmosphere with people suddenly appearing and disappearing with disembodied voices echoing eerily from across the field. As I wandered, I noticed a large board propped up and divided into many squares.

'What's that?' I asked the young farmer in charge.

'Well, you see that field next door,' the mist suddenly swirled away in a patch, and I could see where he pointed. The neighbouring field had an area cordoned off with ropes, and a large cow was being held just on the other side of them.

'A contestant will place a bet on one of the squares on the board, and we have divided the cordoned-off area of that field to correspond.' The young man grinned at me; 'As soon as people have finished betting, Charlie over there will drive Blossom the cow into the roped-off part of the field.'

I had a feeling I knew what was coming.

'As soon as she lets go a dollop, the person whose bet is on the nearest square on my board to where it lands, gets a prize.'

I decided not to ask what the prize was.

The whole 'Event' is slightly zany: but visitors might ask, 'What else would you expect on Sark?'

There are other carnivals and fund-raising events that occur on a regular basis on the Island. The need to replenish funds in the Professor Saint Trust and other needy charities ensures that there will always be a constant effort by Island residents to raise money. It has been said that 'per capita' more charity money is raised on the Island than most places of a similar population.

Coffee mornings, jumble sales and a 'Sark Carnival' (different from the Water Carnival and usually held in August) all add finance to services that most residents may need at one time or another.

The Sark Carnival mainly consisted of stalls selling anything from used books to home-made cakes. There were several tombolas and activities for children, like bobbing for apples or trying to hook a plastic duck floating in a tub of water. There would also be several food tents, with barbecued sausages and meats, cakes, sandwiches, and of course a beer tent. This last has caused a few problems for the constables. It has become an invitation for the off-Island binge-drinkers to overindulge and spoil the day for others and the event has had to be changed over the years.

I was happy to offer my help, and usually ended up in the food tent. I really enjoyed meeting the visitors, though sometimes I had some strange comments from them.

'It's a nice little Island,' said one young woman as she picked up her cup of tea, 'but what do you DO all the time?'

I thought for a moment and then said, 'Well, I suppose much the same as everyone else: but rather more of it!'

I had every reason to make that comment. As well as carnivals, coffee mornings and jumble sales, there are the garden and produce shows. The 'Midsummer Show' is held in June, and the 'Autumn Show' is in September. The June one is more geared to gardens, flowers and vegetables, while the later one includes farm produce and home-made cakes, jams, chutneys and such delights.

The competition is fierce, and for weeks people closely guard their special flowers and vegetables. I enjoyed entering several classes, and learned how anxious one could become in the few days before show day. It always seemed that nature was against the exhibitors: the rain and wind could devastate the perfect rose: bugs get into the vegetables, or the tidy garden suddenly scorch brown or run wild. Entries had to be put in about a week before the show, and it was very difficult to determine which flower would be in a perfect condition come the day.

Exhibitors brought their prized contributions by bicycle or pushing a wheelbarrow: a few used a tractor, but of course there are no cars to make life easy. Once at the Island Hall you wandered around until you found the allocated place for your exhibit. You then filled the vase with water or placed the fruit or vegetables in an artistic display, making sure you had the exact number required. After once taking only the number of roses I thought I needed, and damaging one on the way, I always took a few extras to avoid that frantic dash home to replace it.

Finally the items were judged by experts brought in from Guernsey or Jersey: a local person would be out of the question if there were any points of dispute. The retribution would have been worthy of the TV series 'Midsummer Murders.'

We exhibitors would queue outside the hall and rush in as soon as the doors were opened. We would saunter around looking at the other exhibits with a nonchalance belying our keenness to discover any awards we had ourselves. The thrill in discovering a coloured 'first', 'second' or 'third' card by our own precious contribution was equal to that felt as a child when you had a good result from a classroom exam.

**An entry for the Water Carnival and
Chris in the Cavalcade**

21

During the June Flower Show, Islanders were encouraged to enter their gardens to be judged. The classes varied from cottage to large gardens, and it was from one of these Shows that Peter and I had a brainwave. We were amazed to discover that there were often 13 to 20 people who offered their gardens for judging.

Peter's daughter Ann was a keen follower of the 'Yellow Book' system of open gardens in England and we often accompanied her to some of them when we visited her.

One day, soon after we had returned from such a trip, we were having lunch in our own garden. It had matured in the eight years or so since we had renovated Camp Farm and had we entered it in the recent show and received a second prize.

'What do you think of organising something like the Yellow Book system here?' Peter asked me as he put his glass of beer down on the table.

'That sounds like a great idea: but how on earth to get people interested?'

We talked it over with a few friends, and the outcome was a public meeting, which surprised us by being quite well attended. There was a lot of discussion, and most people liked the general idea.

'Can't say I want to be hanging around all day, though, for a few people who might drop in,' one person voiced the general opinion. Then someone came up with the idea of a guided walk.

'Maybe visitors could meet, say outside the Island hall and some of us take them to a few gardens?'

Gradually the ideas grew and at the end of the meeting, the basic plan for 'The Sark Garden Walks' was established.

In 1994, a group of four, Peter, myself, and two Islanders, Debbie Guille and June Caree, formed the first 'committee,' and we continued to worked together for many years. Gradually we developed a formula and refined it into a working system. The basic idea was to divide the Island into three areas where people were willing to open their gardens for us to bring walkers on a specific day and at a specific time. We fixed one day of the week, starting soon after Easter and usually offering the last walk in mid-September. In each area there could be up to eight gardens available, but we decided that six would be enough to visit each time, as there could be a lot of walking between. That meant that not every garden in each area would be needed every third week in roster, so it was not too demanding a task to present a tidy garden. We said to gardeners: 'We tell people that these are not show gardens, just like yours, to share. Please don't rush around tidying everything up:' but of course we all did.

In the Yellow Book system there was some refreshment for sale, but we decided that our overall charge (which was minimal and went to charity) should include a cup of tea and a biscuit at the last garden. It proved difficult to restrict the generous hosts to stick to just biscuits and many provided home-made cakes and buns.

We decided that two guides would be needed each week. A few days before the walk, the main guide would be responsible for notifying the garden owners to be visited and reminding the other guide and tea-stop. This person would also need to be able to chat with the walkers and ideally know a little about gardening and any interesting stories about the Island.

The second, or 'sweeper' was needed to try and keep the group from straggling and make sure no-one was left behind.

On some occasions this proved quite difficult when people wanted to have a lengthy discussion with one of the gardeners.

I remember one walk when half the party disappeared and never did catch up with the main group.

What started as a bright idea soon became complicated and involved a lot of work for us all. Gardeners had to be cajoled into agreeing to open their gardens: tea stops had to be found that could accommodate up to 40 people if it started to rain: volunteer guides cajoled, and walking routes discussed, as we wanted to make them as interesting as possible.

We four used to get together well before starting day over a cup of coffee at one of our homes and battle it out.

'You can't put Vicky as 'sweeper' with Tom as a main guide, they don't get on:'

'Look, Angela's garden is put down for four visits and Becky's for only two:'

'We need another tea-stop in the East group: we only have two: can't expect them to do too many.'

'We will have to try and get another garden in the North group, we just don't have enough, and we have too many in the West group: maybe we can switch one around:'

And so on.

We did not want to be too regimented, but it was necessary to suggest a few 'do's' and 'don'ts'. Some guides charged ahead, giving walkers no time to browse, while others spent too much time chatting to the few at the head of the group. Decisions had to be made if more than 40 people turned up: we never knew how many people would meet at the designated starting place, as we did not request pre-booking. Occasionally we had to split the route and send one group clockwise while the others went the other way, meeting at the tea-stop. It was also the main guide's job to phone the tea stop hostess just before departure, with the number of walkers and occasionally they forgot.

Eventually I found myself having to write and duplicate several notifications: the route roster: the guides' names for each walk: lists of contact phone numbers: and a few instructions for the guides. What started out as a simple idea, blossomed almost to a military exercise.

We also learned a few things along the way, in particular regarding insurance. We thought it was sufficient to announce at the beginning of each walk that we took no responsibility for any accidents, but we were informed that we needed a proper insurance. After the first three walks, when things could have gone very wrong, we acted on that advice.

On the first walk, when I was the main guide and Peter the sweeper, a very pregnant woman decided to join us. I tried to dissuade her, as the walk was several miles and covered rough ground: but she would not listen.

Inevitably half-way through, her husband pushed his way to the front:

'You've got to get the ambulance: I think my wife is going into labour. This walk is too much for her: you really should have warned us!' I refrained from the obvious comment, and ran to the nearest house to telephone the doctor.

I was also on the second and third walks, not guiding but just for the experience. During one walk someone was stung by a bee, and on the other a person had an asthma attack. Fortunately no-one held us liable, but it could have been different.

We did little advertising of the Walks, as they were almost too successful. We had to learn to refuse tour groups who wanted to put the walk on their itinerary. We did accept one or two, until it became out of hand. One tour company who brought some Americans expected us to organise a carriage trip and afternoon tea: we politely refused.

To my great surprise, and I admit satisfaction, the Sark Garden Walks have survived for over 20 years: they have become 'Something not to be missed, on a Sark visit.'

A spin-off from our work with Sark's gardens was the involvement in a few television programmes. One company in particular visited the Island several times, and we were fortunate to have a part of it filmed in our garden at Camp Farm. The format included a visit to the Seigneurie gardens where the public could ask gardening questions. Then a special 'gardening tip' was discussed and demonstrated by one of the filming personalities. Ideas had to be sent to the film company before-hand and one that I submitted was chosen.

I used to cut up my laddered stockings and tights to make ties for my plants and young trees when fixing them to stakes. After slicing off the toe, I cut across each leg in half-inch rings: these I held with my fingers and cut again to make a tie. The body part was done the same way to make bigger ties, and the crotch that was left became useful as support for the fruit when we grew melons in our small lean-to greenhouse.

A well-known personality, who had been a bit of a 'playboy' in his time, was to demonstrate this 'tip' and I was interested to meet him.

We sat in our conservatory as I demonstrated my technique, but I noticed that he was looking around at our passion-fruit vine and lemon tree.

'You're not looking!'

'Yes I am, my dear,' and he proceeded to do exactly as I had shown him.

To film the melon part, the crew had partially to dismantle the greenhouse so that they could get the cameras in: they put it all back afterwards.

While the cameras were set up, the 'personality' picked up one of the melon supports and bounced it under a melon;

'If I was a melon, I'd love that.'

'You can't say that!'

'No, but it would liven things up a bit.'

Despite all the joking the team were totally professional and I felt very privileged to see them at work.

Another Island activity that I became involved in through the Garden Walks was with 'Floral Sark'. Every year there was a nation-wide competition to choose the most attractive village or parish and it was decided to groom Sark to be an entrant. Several of the Guernsey parishes took part, and we were determined to beat them if possible.

A group of us met on a regular basis, but it was Caroline Langford who ran the Gallery Stores, who was the leading light. Her dedication and energy was infectious and most of the Island became involved.

The judging was not just on floral displays but on the appearance of the whole parish, or Island in this case. Such things as the participation of the residents, cleanliness and lack of rubbish and even the involvement of the children at school were taken into account.

For weeks we met and planned over a cup of tea and discussed such things as the replacement of rubbish bins: planting of trees and flowers: island-wide rubbish pick-up groups and ways of enhancing the natural beauty of Sark. We all decided that the Island had enough natural attraction without adorning it with hanging baskets and bright flower beds.

I had always been aware that some of the visitors seemed unable to wait until finding a waste-paper bin to dispose of their picnic papers. I now became almost paranoid about picking up any rubbish as I cycled around, carrying a plastic bag with me to use. I was not averse to chasing after someone and handing the chocolate wrapper back to them.

'This is yours, I think!'

All the effort was worth it as we won several awards, both locally and nationally.

22

Although I had some nursing, and was involved with community activities, I became a little restless: I felt I needed some mental stimulation. It was Peter who first drew my attention to an article in the local paper.

'Have you seen this Chris? 'All about homeopathy.' There is an advert for something called the 'British Institute of Homeopathy,' where you can do a correspondence course.'

I leant over Peter's shoulder and peered at the article. I became quite excited: for many years I had been interested in the subject and had used a few homeopathic remedies in the past.

'It would mean a lot of study: and I might have to go away for a week or so occasionally.'

At that, Peter was not very happy. I loved him dearly, but his possessiveness sometimes concerned me. He hated me to be away from him: when I visited my mother he phoned every day, and he resented my going to Holland to see my brother, or to Roy and Annette after they moved to Sweden to continue their University studies. When I tackled him once about that, his reply floored me.

'Well, after all you left Ken: you might do the same to me, and I couldn't bear that.'

I put my arms tightly round him and promised that would never happen, but I knew deep down he was still insecure. There was much of the 'little boy' about Peter: as I loved him so much it did not matter to me if he sometimes acted a little like a spoiled child. Once I had been to see Roy and Annette on my own as Peter was unable to go. I brought him a special present, but he was totally uninterested in it. His greeting, once we were in our bedroom was almost overwhelming in its intensity.

I wrote to the address in the advertisement and in no time I was enrolled as a student for a Diploma with the

240

British Institute of Homeopathy. Each student was allocated a personal tutor, and as luck would have it a homeopath in Alderney agreed to be mine.

It was a very exacting course, involving the purchase of books: essays to be written and marked: visits to Alderney for tutorials, and practical experience. I had become totally unused to the discipline of study, and my tutor told me after I had qualified, that she had wondered if I would make it.

'Chris, your first essays were not really up to scratch: but once you got going . . .well there was no holding you!'

I rediscovered the pleasure of study and had not really thought about having a practice of my own until my tutor suggested I consider it. It had only taken me a year to get my first Diploma, and I was delighted to be made a 'Fellow of the B.I.H' because of my high marks.

'Why not take the advanced Medical Diploma?' My tutor urged, 'I would be happy to be your tutor for that too.'

So I took her advice and continued studying for a further two years. It was a much harder course and to be registered at the end, I had to spend a certain time in other homeopathic clinics: sit in on a set number of consultations and write 25 case studies.

I had thought Peter would be unhappy about my being away for two weeks, but he surprised me.

'I have approached my cousin Evelyn and her husband Don, in Dover. I think you said there are several clinics near there you can attend, so you could stay with them. I can pop over at the week-ends maybe?'

So this is what was arranged, and I had two weeks of travelling to various homeopathic clinics in the area. I had fortunately kept my little Fiat car in England with Peter's daughter Lyn. Clinics were held at all hours, and by travelling from one to another, with sometimes a twelve-hour day I managed to accumulate the necessary hours of experience.

It was November, and the weather was as grey and drizzly as only an English November can be, but I enjoyed the clinics and meeting other homeopaths. One has remained my friend for many years.

I was very grateful to Don and Evelyn for putting up with me. It was so wonderful to return to the warm, comfortable house and friendship, after a tiring long day and freezing drive home along the motorway in the dusky grey light. They are a Christian couple with three delightful sons: I shall be forever in their debt.

Soon after my return to Sark I realised that I wanted to put my knowledge into practice. My exposure to the clinics in the U.K. reinforced my belief in total care of a patient. Throughout my nursing experience I had time and again acknowledged the need to look beyond the medical diagnosis. In taking a homeopathic consultation the practitioner studies every aspect of the patient, from past family history, dietary preferences, sleep and dream patterns, emotional states and bodily functions. During the one and a half hour first consultation, a homeopath will be observing behaviour and appearance and reaction to questioning. At the end, a full picture will emerge, a medical diagnosis is not necessarily of prime importance. Treatment centres around strengthening the person's immune system, so that the body can fight the medical or emotional problem.

It was my experience over the many years I practiced, that much of the help came from the intimate long consultation, where often patients would remark, 'I never told anyone that before.' It was my aim to have a relaxed, comfortable person before I even thought of a remedy that would help the physical or mental problems. Half the healing would already have begun. My experiences as a district nurse in New Zealand, and a course on counselling were of great value.

Eventually, after I had taken other courses including two-years of herbal medicine, I formed my 'Healthy Life Clinics' in Sark and Guernsey. These covered lifestyle advice, diet control, homeopathy, and hair root analysis from a specialist doctor in Wimpole St in London.

That was all in the future. Having decided to practice as a qualified homeopath I needed premises and patients. A friend told me of someone who had a shop in the old part of St Peter Port, Guernsey's main town. It sold Moroccan furniture and pianos, but only on Fridays, Saturdays and Sundays, and they would be happy to rent it for one of the other days of the week.

As I walked up the old cobbles streets, I remembered reading Elizabeth Gouge's 'Green Dolphin Country' set in Guernsey and New Zealand. She wrote of the swirling, buffeting wind skittering down the lanes, and I was transported back a century. The wooden shop-fronts could hardly have changed since that day, and as I approached the one that would be my first clinic rooms, my heart skipped a beat. There was a large bowed window facing down the hill, with green-painted woodwork. It did not look like a clinic, but when I put up some copies of my certificates and a notice, it looked more the part.

It was hard work at first and the shop was not ideal. I had to buy a screen to give some privacy from the passers-by, and there was no waiting area. If my next patients arrived before I had finished the previous one, they had to stand outside. It was a very quiet part of town and as I sometimes gave an evening consultation, I felt a little vulnerable.

This was brought home on one such occasion. I had made an appointment one evening for a young man who said he worked during the day. When this happened, I usually stayed in a small bed and breakfast place nearby as there were no evening boats back to Sark.

When the patient arrived I became a little alarmed. He was shaven-headed, with tattoos and piercings, but his manner was quite pleasant.

As I usually did, I started my consultation by asking my patient what he felt was his problem.

'Well, I have just come out of prison. . . a little drug misunderstanding, you might say.' I sat uncomfortably twiddling my pen thinking I could be in trouble.

'I want to do better with my life: my sister Jinny you saw a couple of months ago, said you did wonders for her. She nagged me to come and see you.' He sat with his arms folded.

'Well, what do you think I can do? Do you want to get off drugs?'

'I'm just about clean now, but I get these night sweats and a rash.'

Now we were talking my language and gradually I took a history, realising he was the same as all my other patients. He needed reassurance and support as much as medication, and as with all my patients I told him he could phone me if he had problems. He did on a regular basis for nearly six months.

Gradually this young man improved: he went to night school. The last I heard he was working among drug addicts in the East End of London. It may not have been pure homeopathy, but it worked.

23

After our holidays in Scotland and New Zealand, Peter and I discussed other places we would like to visit. Peter had obviously been giving it some thought.

'How would you like to go on safari?'

'Where?'

'Well I thought Kenya. I got a few brochures from a company I heard of, from that travel agent I use for the Music Council bookings.'

I had always wanted to visit Africa but was a little afraid of being close to the wild animals, especially elephants. I had not enjoyed zoos as a child. I thought it so cruel to restrict the animals and the hugeness of the elephants in close proximity made me aware of the restrained power that was barely contained.

Peter showed me one brochure by a company that took small groups.

'They are a bit more expensive, but you don't go around in convoys of sightseers.'

'Oh, yes I'd love that: it sounds fantastic.'

'Then I thought we might have a few days recovery in an island called Lamu, just off the coast. What do you think?'

'That's going to be a bit expensive.' I had still not become used to Peter's generosity and my new lifestyle that allowed for such exciting holidays. I was cautious after years of making do when running our guest house and then in New Zealand where we lived off my salary.

Peter put his arms round me and gave a big hug: 'It is good to have someone to spend my money on.' I still thrilled to Peter's touch and warmth. He was so enthusiastic and alive: you could not help but be affected by his vitality.

The booking went ahead without a hitch, and it was soon the end of January and time to start on our way. Departure from Sark in winter for a holiday was always fraught. For days before we kept a sharp eye on the weather forecast. Any suggestion of strong winds meant an early departure, as there could be trouble getting the boat into the Sark harbour. We had decided to spend a night in Guernsey at our favourite hotel in St Peter Port: fly to London and spend another few days there and finally meet the tour advisor to receive the last of the safari details.

I had been having a niggling toothache for a few days, but hoped it would settle. On the morning of departure, I woke with an ache over the whole of one side of my face. I had worked with a dentist in London just after qualifying as a nurse, and suspected I had a tooth abscess.

I was fortunate to get an appointment at my surgery in Guernsey, but it was not my usual dentist, and he was not very helpful.

'No: I don't think it is an abscess. Probably an infected sinus. I'll give you some antibiotics.'

The dentist refused to do an x-ray and dismissed me, suggesting I come back if it did not get better. I had told him I was on my way to Africa, but he did not seem interested.

By the time we booked into our London hotel I was feeling far from well. We had been to this small private hotel just off Curzon Street before and got to know the doorman. As I walked in, he greeted us as usual, then showed some concern at my swollen face.

'If you need a dentist, Madam, if you don't mind my saying so, my cousin has a practice not far from here: I could get you an appointment I am sure if I put a word in.'

He was as good as his word, and within a few hours I was sitting in a dentist's chair again.

'You are quite right, Mrs Curtis: it is an abscess. I will have to do a root canal drain.'

It was a most unpleasant start to our holiday, but I dreaded to think what would have happened if I had gone to Africa without treatment. I now realised the importance of advice the travel agent had given us to buy an emergency medical kit from a place in Regents Street. With the prevalence of AIDS in Africa, medical treatment could be very dangerous. The pack contained sterile needles, a transfusion set, syringes and dressings. There was also a card for you to write your contact phone numbers, your blood group and details of next of kin. We had already had vaccinations for typhoid, yellow fever and hepatitis and started anti-malaria pills. My preference for complementary medicine warred in my mind with a need for self-preservation and I was beginning to wonder what I was getting myself into.

By the next day I felt much better: the pressure had been relieved, a temporary filling was in place, and the antibiotics were working. I was able to enjoy a show we had booked and manage a delightful late dinner at a Turkish restaurant in Shepherd's Market, just round the corner from our hotel. We had discovered this tucked-away pocket of small eating places on our walk back from the dentist. They advertised 'Late Dining After Your Show,' so we decided to book for ten thirty.

True to their word, we were served a wonderful Turkish meal, with many small dishes following one after the other until well after midnight. When all the other customers had left, the owners came over to our table, chatted and gave us several free sweet liqueurs. They were very interested to hear about the strange little feudal island of Sark, and we had to drag ourselves away by three in the morning. We were glad the hotel was just round the corner as the drinks had been strong and generously offered.

After a late start and meeting the tour representative, at last we were on our way to Nairobi. The flight was longer than I had expected but any tiredness went when we were met by private car and driven to the luxurious 'Norfolk Hotel.' We were to spend our first night there and meet our safari driver and the other people in the group. It was my first visit to a 'third world' country and I was sad to see all the evidence of poverty as we drove through the streets: little boys running by the side of the taxi banging on the window for money: the beggars sitting in shop doorways and the shacks by the side of the road. I wanted to give the boys some small change but the driver shook his head:

'Don ya open ya window missis; you give they little brats money: they go buy petrol to sniff.'

When we arrived at the hotel I felt almost guilty, but determined to enjoy every moment and soon the excitement took over.

'I wonder who will be with us in the party?' Peter voiced my predominating thought. We knew there would not be more than six of us in the mini-bus, but we would be together for several days. We would be staying at the same hotels and touring together. We had both had unfortunate experiences with tourists who had no consideration of others in a group.

We need not have worried. Lee and Mini Chang added much to our enjoyment throughout the trip. There were only the four of us, and after the first shyness we became firm friends.

'I 'ad much worry you smoke.' Mini confided to us later.

'Well, we did too.'

Lee and Mini were living in America, but Mini did not speak much English, though she understood most things. She developed a love of the funny little warthogs that ran through the bush with stiff tails aloft. As soon as any of us saw one we'd say 'Look Mini warhogg; warhogg!' She could not pronounce her 'ts.'

That first trip to Africa lit a special light in my heart. I had heard it was possible to fall in love with this hot arid land full of danger and discomfort: and I was surprised that it happened to me.

To go out in the vehicle early in the morning and just park with the engine off and watch the sun rise was magic. To listen to the collared doves cooing from the acacia trees and shiver to the distant roar of a lion: to watch the tottering of a new-born wilderbeest calf and search in the long grass for the sight of a long-eared fox or ocelot was an excitement I had never dreamed was possible.

Our driver Andrew was an expert spotter and gave us many tips. We were told later that he used to drive for royal visitors when he was younger and was one of the best.

'You see the zebras are all facing one way? Follow where they're looking: do you see anything?' Sure enough you would see a pair on amber eyes peering through the long grass: a lioness was hunting.

'I stopped to let this group of elephants all go across the road. Never split a family: you'd be in real trouble.'

'Don't get out of the vehicle near hippos: they are very dangerous and can travel really fast.'

24

We stayed at two different hotels, one in the Amboseli Park and the other in the Serengeti, which were far more luxurious than I had imagined. One had a swimming pool and both had top quality restaurants.

The highlight was a night at 'The Ark' in the Aberdare National Park, which gave us an experience of a lifetime. This unique hotel-cum-safari park lodge was situated by a huge waterhole. The building was wooden, and as our minibus approached it certainly looked like the proverbial Noah's Ark with its curved roof and boat-like appearance. Inside it was as luxurious as the other two hotels, and everything was geared to observing the animals that visited the waterhole. There was a huge deck and several observation rooms. The bedrooms were not very large and had small windows.

'Well you won't be spending much time there,' Andrew told us. 'If something interesting happens at the waterhole in the night, they ring a bell so you can go and see. Some people stay up all night anyway.'

In fact Peter and I did not have much sleep.

'I don't want to miss anything. I don't expect we will come here again.' I was glad I stayed up until late, as a young rhino calf and its mother arrived soon after sunset, and did not seem to be worried by the spotlights round the pool: but by midnight I could not stay awake any longer.

It seemed no sooner had I drifted off to sleep, than I was woken by the bell ringing. Sleepily I tumbled out of bed thinking I was a district nurse back in New Zealand and the phone was ringing to summon me to go on a night call.

A large herd of elephants had arrived at the waterhole and as I sleepily looked at them, out of the corner of my eye I saw a flash of movement in the shadows. I was fully awake by then and grabbed Peter's arm.

'Did you see that? I think it was a leopard.'

We both peered into half-light, and sure enough we saw the gleam of a spotted coat moving slowly back into the darkness.

'Wow: I wonder if anyone else saw it?' There were about twenty others on the deck, but they all seemed to be looking at the elephants.

At breakfast the next morning it appeared we were the only ones that had seen the leopard.

'I am proud of you,' said Andrew.

Our time on safari was too short, but after ten days I had to admit I was pretty tired. Most days we had to get up early for a dawn drive, the best time to see the animals, as by midday the big cats sought shade: the giraffes disappeared under the acacia trees and the smaller animals hid in the long grass.

I was sorry to say goodbye to Andrew but looked forward to our stay in the 'Pepone Hotel' on Lamu Island. There was a short flight from Nairobi airport in such a small plane that the Inter Island 'Trylander' planes back home seemed large. We then had to board an overcrowded ferry to the smaller Island that was to be our home for a week.

Situated right on the beach, and with an outdoor theme, it was the perfect foil for the strenuous safari we had just left. Out bedroom, called the 'Top-Room' was just that. Spread over a large deck and bedroom on the top floor, it had views over the neighbouring village and sea. Outside under a half-roof a double hammock offered a choice from the huge four-poster bed inside. It was absolute bliss: the food was fresh and abundant. We watched the owner of the hotel each morning haggling with the fishermen below us on the beach and delighted in seeing the little donkeys loaded with fresh fruit and vegetables plodding by. The beach was used as a road, as there appeared to be few vehicles and the interior roads were unmade.

We did not explore the village, feeling lazy after the strenuous safari, but did hire one of the local dhows to visit some other villages and islands nearby. Manned by two local men, these single-sailed boats had changed hardly at all from those used by the ancients. The shape was classic, and I remembered seeing paintings on Egyptian vases, showing the large tapered sail and single float. The crew were as agile as monkeys, running the length of the boat and out onto the float without hesitation.

Ali and Mustafa were Muslim, as were many Kenyans but explained in their excellent English, that they were exempt from responding to prayer call while sailing the dhow; for that we were grateful! We had two excellent days skimming over the water and visiting remote places and villages and became quite attached to our crew. Of course it was expected that a large tip was forthcoming at the end, but we felt they had earned it.

We had been informed by the safari group that wages were very low in Kenya and many people in the tourist industry relied heavily on substantial tips. Having lived in New Zealand where tipping was not a general rule, I did find this a little difficult to accept, but when we visited the villages and saw the basic living conditions, it put a new light on the whole situation.

As the plane lifted away from Nairobi airport, I was sad to leave and vowed to return if at all possible. Peter was of the same mind, and we had a wonderful tented safari in Tanzania a few years later.

As it happened, we were to see Andrew again briefly, then.

When we had been on safari with him, one day we went for a picnic. As we sat on a rug under a huge tree among dried-up elephant droppings, Peter took out our travelling knife and fork set to cut an apple. This neat little kit had also a tin opener and several attachments.

'Hey, that is a useful set: it covers so much that would be useful.' Peter handed it to Andrew to look at and we could see he was very taken with the little gadget. Peter did not want to give it away as it had been a present from me. On our return home we managed to buy another and sent it to Andrew via the safari company.

As we arrived in the entrance lobby of the lovely Norfolk Hotel again in Nairobi before we started our Tanzania trip, we heard our names being called: and there was Andrew. In his hand he held aloft the knife set we had sent. Unmindful of stares I gave him a great hug.

'I take this everywhere with me; thank you: thank you. What are you doing here? You are not with me this time?' We explained that we were on our way to Tanzania.

'You will enjoy that: not very touristy yet.' And he was right. Except for the area between Kenya and Tanzania where we had to stop for passport control, and we were besieged with people trying to sell everything from beads to carvings, it was unspoiled.

This safari was quite different. We were the only people who had booked, so we were totally spoiled with a driver to ourselves and a team of 'boys'(as the cook and his helpers were called) to look after us. The tents were pitched in three different parks, and we stayed in two hotels while the tents went ahead. In the Tarangire, under the lee of Kilimanjaro there had been heavy rain and the flooding added to the excitement. We spent a night in a hotel which had been a farm, and then were driven to the Serengeti, where we spent our second night under canvas. I had never been camping before, but even I realised this was luxury. The camp beds were comfortable and the tents were so big that we could stand up in the centre. I had almost lost my fear of wild animals, but did not take any chances. As our dug-out toilet was separated from the tent, you had to unzip the back of the tent and walk across to it. One night I was about to answer a call of nature and heard a snuffling just the other side of the tent wall by my bed. The 'windows' were just mesh with a zip cover. I looked out, right into the eyes of a hyena. I decide not to go out. The next day our guide laughingly said;

'Oh they are such cowards: you just have to shoo them and they will run away.'

Each day we had a canvas washbowl of hot water, and when we returned tired and hungry, a bottle of whiskey and glasses awaited us: as did a sumptuous meal. I never ceased to marvel at the expertise of the 'boys' who cooked on an open fire. We invited the driver to join us at the evening meal, which he was glad to do. It was Ramadan and as he was Muslim, could not eat between sunrise and sunset.

The final stay was on the edge of the majestic huge Ngorongoro Crater. No-one was allowed to be in the Crater after six in the evening, so we had to stay in the wooded area nearby.

It was magical and our guide almost as good as Andrew. On our very last day he took us down into the Crater and stopped by a large area of reeds and low bush.

'Just watch quietly,' he said

There was a rustling and then one by one, three female lions and eight cubs of varying ages came out of the undergrowth. We could have touched them, we were so close. For a while we were privileged to watch the activities of the family group until it was time to leave the crater.

It was our last day and we were sad to leave Africa again.

'We must come back,' Peter spoke for both of us as we said goodbye to the men who had looked after us so well.

It was not to be however.

Our camp in Tanzania and Elephants

Lions in the Ngorongoro Crater

25

We usually took our holidays in January or February as the Island was often wet and windy. The one time we seldom went away was at Christmas: on Sark the season was always delightful. I felt it was close to how it should be celebrated. The decorations in the Avenue did not appear until December and we were not deafened with tinned carols in all the shops. Naturally the church choir had to start rehearsing early as we had several special services to attend. A week or so before we had the nine lessons and carols: then on Christmas Eve at five p.m. we sang at a 'candlelight service.' When everyone was in the church, the lights were turned off and just one candle burned on the altar. One member of the choir lit a small hand-held candle from this, and then on to another choir member and so on to everyone in the church. People had been given an unlit small candle with a cardboard hand-guard as they entered. It was magic to see the lovely church slowly come to life. On the previous Saturday we women had decorated every nook and cranny with greenery and flowers so this added to the atmosphere.

We had a service at 11pm that night and another at 11 am on Christmas morning. The most enjoyable however, was the Island-wide door-to-door carol singing. This started a week or two before Christmas and was run by a group of dedicated young Islanders. Every house was given the opportunity to receive the singers. Many of the church choir joined but anyone was welcome. The routes were advertised beforehand, and householders could opt out if they wanted. Few did, and several offered refreshment on the way. We were plied with food and drink, sometimes so generously that it was a far from sober group that finally staggered home.

I shall never forget the magic of seeing the lights held high on poles way ahead at the meeting place and hurrying to join the group, hoping they would not move off before I arrived. Although I thought I knew the Island well it was easy to get lost in the dark. We would scramble down bending tracks and across fields to reach houses that I had no idea existed: then we would stand around singing, hoping the rain would keep off. We usually ended the night at one or other house where a special feast had been prepared.

The one in Little Sark was especially wonderful. A lovely Sarkee older couple would invite us in to drink home-made rich soup and consume plates of sausage rolls, mince pies and home-made cake. Carols would be sung and then we had to face the two and a half mile trek back over the Coupee in pitch dark. We all would have torches: no street lights on the Island of course.

One other Island tradition that I was slow to discover occurred on the morning of Christmas Eve. Peter was not in the practice of offering to do the shopping: except on that day. I soon discovered why. Each shop and even the two banks produced food and drink for all its customers if they happened to call in. Few of us even pretended to be there as customers, but the hospitality was offered anyway.

Peter was a great one for traditions. On Christmas Eve, no matter how busy I was, we needs must sit down with a glass of wine, tangerines and listen to the King's College Choir from Cambridge sing carols.

One family tradition that survived long after Pippa and Charlie grew up, was the decorating of our Christmas tree. From a very early age they loved to come over and adorn the tree. Then we would sit down together and watch a recording of 'The Muppets' Christmas' to treats of mince pies and cocoa, or a little alcohol as they grew older.

Christmas day was a busy one for Peter and me. We always had a crowd of people for the dinner. Sometimes it would be all our families, even on occasion Roy and Annette all the way from New Zealand or Sweden. On other occasions we had a self-styled group calling themselves, 'The Waifs and Strays.' There were several people on their own and we were pleased to invite them to Camp Farm. The trouble was that I was never sure how many would come. I had to order the turkey a long time before, so it was difficult to decide how large a one to get. I liked to have a free-range boned one from a special butcher in the Guernsey covered market, and they were hard to come by. One year an unexpected fifteen decided to accept and I had to make up with ham. We really enjoyed the company and after all that is what Christmas is all about.

The festivities did not end with Christmas. Most of the inhabitants would meet to see the New Year in, but it was New Year's Day that brought out the zany side of Sark's residents. Someone always managed to organise some unusual activity for everyone to enjoy. One year it might be a fancy-dress football match; men against women: or a buggy race down Harbour Hill. The ingenuity of the organisers knew no bounds.

Winter was a time for Islanders to socialise. Coffee mornings, jumble sales and Theatre Group productions blossomed. A group of about 40 singers and would-be singers were licked into shape to form the 'Sark Singers' to perform for the public. We were blessed with an ex-professional musician and a very talented young Island man who believed we were capable of four and eight-part renderings. Nothing was rejected as impossible: from local patois songs to Vaughan Williams' song cycles and extracts from church music.

The hall would be packed and I always thought it a shame that we only gave one or two performances. It would have gone down well when there were visitors to the Island in the summer. The problem was that most of the singers were involved one way or another with tourism and would not be able to spare the time.

As soon as Christmas was over the bookings started to roll in for the new season. I was pleased that I was not in the catering business any more, although we had many visits from family and friends, so sometimes I felt I was indeed running a business.

In a mild winter the first primroses might appear around Christmas time, and there was gorse blooming much of the year. Winter aconite starred the banks and a few brave pink campion joined in the pretence that spring was just round the corner. Soon the first daffodils would flower and it was then a downhill run until the first visitors came to stay and Sark put on its summer coat.

<h1 style="text-align:center">26</h1>

Despite holidays and trips away, I was kept busy with patients on Sark and with my growing 'Healthy Life Clinic'. Peter did not mind my weekly trip over to Guernsey but when I was asked to stand in for the doctor he sometimes was not too keen for me to accept: especially if it conflicted with any plans we had made. I know it was partly because I became anxious when I was 'on call' as it was such a responsibility and I 'switched to my nursing mode', as he put it. I had reason to be anxious, as a nursing friend in Guernsey pointed out; despite my Royal College of Nursing insurance cover I was very vulnerable to litigation.

This was brought home to me in no uncertain way during one overnight 'on call' session. A middle-aged lady, living with her sister in Little Sark had a fall at home and I was asked to see her. I knew the woman was prone to confusion, but her reactions and state concerned me when I examined her.

By this time the doctor had a mobile phone, so I contacted him and said I thought she should go on the ambulance launch to the Guernsey hospital.

'Oh, Chris; she is always falling, and you know she has mild dementia. Leave it to the morning and see how she is.'

I was not happy but went by the doctor's decision, but early next morning the sister phoned in distress.

'Chris I am so worried, Fanny fell again and I can't rouse her.' I was there as fast as my bike would take me: even riding part-way across La Coupee which was discouraged.

There was no doubt that the patient was much worse, so I ordered an ambulance and told the doctor afterwards.

The patient died in the hospital, from a sub-dural haemorrhage.

Soon afterwards the doctor asked me to call into the surgery and I was alarmed to see a policeman from Guernsey with him.

'It's alright, Chris: don't worry, but you will need to make a statement for the coroner. There was a lot of scarring on her brain from previous falls, so it was just a matter of time before this happened.'

I wrote the whole story down as it had occurred, and there were no repercussions: but it caused me a few sleepless nights and I had to think seriously about my situation. I think the doctor was a concerned for me too, as I was not asked so often to take an overnight 'locum' after that.

I had several other patients that I thoroughly enjoyed seeing. One very elderly lady became a 'regular.' She was not keen on calling a doctor, so whenever she had a problem I would get a phone call.

'Hello, Christine: when you are next down this way could you just call in, do you think, please?' She was from a well-to-do family and was reserved about her personal female problems. She had a recurring discomfort which I was able to relieve. After treatment we developed a ritual.

'Do join me for a sherry my dear:' which would be brought to us on a silver tray in crystal glasses, in the garden in summer and the beautifully furnished lounge in the winter in front of a roaring log fire.

They were a couple from the old school and still called each other by their unabbreviated Christian names. After many years of devoted marriage, sadly the husband developed dementia or Alzheimer's disease as we now call it. I would get calls at all hours of day and night to help persuade the old man, dressed only in his pyjamas to come in from the garden. He loved to wander through the lawns and glades, and when he finally died, his widow laid him to rest in one of his favourite places in the garden.

'Well, Christine, there is no law to say I cannot do that, is there?'

I felt it was a privilege to serve these Island residents and sometimes they were people I had known since my guest house days in the 1960s. One was the aunt of a friend who had moved to Guernsey. One day I was on the boat back to Sark, my friend came over to sit with me.

'Chris, I've been meaning to ask you. You may know Auntie Heather has cancer. . .'

'Yes I had heard: I am so sorry: she was always such a livewire.'

'Yes, well: she won't come over to Guernsey for me to look after her. She is determined to stay at home.'

I thought of the old cottage Heather lived in with outside sanitation and water collected from a tap in the yard. I knew her daughter lived in Jersey and was soon expecting her first child.

I was worried by what was coming but had to ask.

'What do you want me to do?'

'Could you keep an eye on her, d'you think? She can look after herself at the moment and people go in to take food and so on, but I can't stay over there: I have my boys to think of.'

I already had several patients on daily visits but I could only say 'yes.' Heather and her husband had been our 'carters' when my husband Ken and I arrived new to the Island.

They had helped us settle in, delivering groceries and collecting guests' luggage. After her husband's death Heather had valiantly carried on the carting and carriage business.

For several weeks I called in when I could to check Heather was coping, and at first she managed to feed her geese and look after herself. I hated the geese chasing me across her front yard and used to amuse Heather when I dived into the cottage, slamming the door against the ferocious beaks.

'They'll get you one day, Chris.'

As I became less busy with other patients and to get Heather used to me in a more intimate way I tried to stay a little longer in my visits. I knew the time was approaching when my patient would need more personal care.

One day as we were sitting by the fire sipping our cups of coffee, Heather suddenly laughed. 'You know, Chris you caused quite a stir when news came that you and Peter Curtis were going to live together. The stories I heard...!'

'What do you mean?'

'Oh, that Curtis had met a nurse in New Zealand, and she has seduced him and pushed his wife Marjorie out of their marriage.'

I felt a little sick. I had no idea of those stories and was thankful that I had not when I returned to Sark: I doubt otherwise whether I would have had the courage to return.

'Well, of course, when I heard your name, I had to chuckle: and anyway everyone knew that the Curtis' were not getting along too well. After all, he was living in the little cottage and she was in the main house.'

Not for the first time I was aware of the power of gossip on this small Island. I had noticed one or two cold receptions from people I had known before but thought little of it at the time.

'Anyway, you stuck it out and a good thing for Sark is all I can say.'

I reached over and squeezed Heather's hand. I was fond of this gutsy lady and was very sad that she would not be with us much longer: I was determined to keep her at home as she wanted, if at all possible.

Heather's deterioration was rapid, and soon she was unable to leave her bed for long. I managed to visit twice a day, often needing to light the fire and get her some breakfast before boiling water and giving her a wash. But she was content, and people called in to keep her company. Her niece from Guernsey came over as often as she could and when I was expecting her I tended to miss the afternoon visit.

One day I shall not forget, I visited in the morning as usual, but as her niece was going to spend the afternoon with Heather and I had several other patients, I said I would not call.

'Please Chris, do pop in if you can: there is something. .' She had to stop with a coughing fit. I patted her hand, and said I would try.

Sadly I did not manage to call in, and it was the last time I saw Heather alive. She died that night.

When I called to perform last offices. . .something I regularly did. . . Heather's niece was still there.

She handed me a package: 'Auntie wanted to give this to you herself, but just didn't make it. I brought it over yesterday.'

Inside the package was an engraved picture of geese, running with beaks outstretched and wings wide. Underneath she had had inscribed 'Watch out for your heels Chrys.'

It has remained one of my prized possessions, complete with the miss-spelling of my name.

With the passing years, the doctor and his lovely wife had become friends with Peter any me. Gradually Anthea had changed the fenced-in corner of a field, where the new Medical Centre and their house stood, to a garden I was delighted to include in the Garden Walks.

Anthea and I sometimes chatted on the phone, so I was not altogether surprised when she rang me one morning although it was very early. I knew they were usually early risers.

'Oh, Chris, can you come round. Mitch thinks he's had a heart attack.'

I quickly dressed and raced round to the Medical Centre which was not far away.

Mitch certainly looked very ill and I did not need to see his ECG that he had taken to realise there had been a cardiac incident. Together we arranged the St John ambulance launch and his entry to the Hospital in Guernsey.

'You'll have to contact the Seigneur and the Medical Committee: they will have to arrange a locum: do you think you can hold the fort?'

'That's OK: don't you worry, we'll arrange something. Just get well.'

It was a while before Mitch was allowed to return: heart surgery and aftercare were necessary. In the meantime the Sark Medical Committee contacted several doctors in Guernsey who had acted as locum in the past when Mitch and Anthea went away on holiday.

I was asked to look after the practice in between doctors. As it was peak holiday time I was kept pretty busy, but fortunately there were no major incidents like carriage accidents: a not unknown occurrence. One locum was a retired cardiac specialist and used to say that visits to Sark were a 'rest-cure.' He normally came in the winter when Mitch and Anthea preferred to go away for some winter sun. On this occasion the specialist came over to Sark on the August Bank Holiday: one of the busiest weekends in the year.

He called me in to do a few visits, and I was amused by his comment:

'I'll never rib Mitch again: I've never been so rushed. I didn't realise how much was involved here: not only two surgeries each day, but all your own dispensing and being on call 24 hours a day! We Guernsey doctors thought this was a cushy number.'

We were very happy to have Mitch back again with us. He was a very experienced practitioner and had been used to performing minor operations in his previous location. A doctor on Sark needed to be a good 'all-rounder:' he had to be able to diagnose any and every sort of problem: be proficient in obstetrics: be able to order, prescribe and dispense his medicines and know how to use the increasing number of machines available. . .including a computer.

In one of our conversations I mentioned that I had run an out-patients' minor ops theatre in a London hospital before doing my district training.

'How would you like to assist me sometimes then, Chris?' I said I would be delighted, and so that was added to my responsibilities, and I really enjoyed it. I had been missing my New Zealand district nursing practice at first, but gradually found quite enough to do on Sark, with this addition; my nursing visits; occasional locum and my practice in Guernsey.

For all his tendency to possessiveness Peter was proud of my nursing I think, but we made sure we had time for each other. He was often busy with office work, but we managed to go down to one of the beaches as often as we could.

As Port du Moulin, a stony but interesting beach, was just a short walk from Camp Farm we sometimes took a packed lunch down there. It was a lovely walk down a wooded valley across a stream on an old plank bridge.

Down the inevitable steps we went and always delighted in the vista of the giant 'Autelets Rocks': the rock arch and the distant views of Guernsey. There were always gulls circling and crying, but we learned to hide our lunch after one occasion.

We were sitting on a rock eating our sandwiches and an adult gull with its grown chick were hopping near Peter. Suddenly the adult rushed up to Peter and he swung his sandwich away behind him, whereby the chick grabbed it from his hand and flew off with it.

We both had to laugh at the audacity.

There was a lot of laughter in my life with Peter. He told so many jokes and was so full of energy and life. The shock with Mitch made me very aware of how fragile life could be, but the thought of a future without the man I had learned to love so much made me almost sick with panic.

I tried not to think about something that I knew I could not control, although it was constantly in my prayers. While I would not call myself 'religious,' I have felt a presence throughout my life and firmly believe in a loving, though not predictable God. At a risk of seeming casual, I have been prone to 'arrow prayers:' a sort of one-sided conversation on my part.

I sometimes found myself in St Peter's Church when there was no-one else there and the arrow prayers were constantly launched from my heart. Besides attending choir practice each Thursday and Church on Sundays, every few weeks Peter and I had undertaken to be on the 'Church-opening' roster. This responsibility came about as a result of the current Vicar living some distance from the church. So it was that we volunteered to collect the large cast-iron key in the morning to open the church, and lock it up at night. It was not an onerous duty, and as there were at least six people on the roster, we were not called upon often. In summer we opened quite early and closed later at night. I used to love the silence of the early and late hours, disturbed only by a distant bird's call or the clip-clop of a horse going by. I felt a deep peace settle into my heart, and my arrow prayers would be ones of thanks.

There were a few amusing times: suddenly getting ready for bed and one of us asking: 'Did you lock the church?' Followed by an impolite exclamation; a quick pulling on of jeans over night attire and a moonlit cycle-ride quickly to do the job.

Once I arrived to lock up, and just checked to make sure no-one was inside. There was a lady sitting in a pew, bowed over apparently in prayer: I cycled round the block: she was still at prayer. After the third circuit I ventured into the church and cleared my throat: she started up, blushing.

'Oh, dear, I must have dropped off: it is so peaceful here!'

St Peter's Church

28

Our holidays were not always to exotic places. We had met an interesting American couple while we were walking the Milford Track in New Zealand on a previous visit. We had enjoyed their company so much when we shared our cabins with them. There was much laughter especially as Peter and James hated to walk over the many suspension bridges and we watched them trying them out with cautious steps. Their teenage son was also with them and his parents were always teasing him which added to the fun.

We kept in touch and when they invited us in the late 1990s to visit them in Kalamazoo, in Michigan, we jumped at the chance. My only experience of the United States was to visit Disneyland with Roy when he was younger and I was keen to discover more.

The flight was quite long, and for once Peter did not seem his cheerful self, complaining of sinus trouble, but as soon as we met our friends he brightened.

Their home was just as I had imagined from films: made of wood and with grass up to the house with no fences, and large shady trees all the way up the road. They were a very fit couple and lived an outdoor life.

We spent a few days in the delightful town of Kalamazoo and then James surprised us one morning.

'Say, I guess you should see something more than this town. We've borrowed our friend's people-carrier and are going to take you up the coast of Lake Michigan. We have a friend on Drummond Island who has built a most unusual house: we have a standing invite to go see him.'

'We could go visit Mackinac Island too.' Hagar added, as we sat discussing the trip. 'You will find it not unlike your Island of Sark. They don't have many vehicles and use horses for pulling drays and some carriages.'

We drove up the coast of this huge inland lake: I remembered from school days that it was one of the five

'Great Lakes' on the border with Canada. It looked like a sea and the shores had sandy beaches. One bright clear morning we saw clouds of Monarch butterflies circling.

'They know autumn is coming on: you can feel the coolness in the mornings.'

Despite the weather and interesting scenery Peter was still not as well as usual.

'Must be an infected sinus,' he said as he massaged the side if his face. 'I may have to get some antibiotics.'

The stay on Drummond Island was marred a little by Peter's ill-health, but he managed to get some antibiotics, and seemed to recover quite well, except that he complained of a tingling in his hand; he shook it and said 'Must have slept on it.'

The friend's house was certainly unusual. Hexagonal in shape, it was built right on the water's edge, with a wood surrounding the back area. Inside, the centre was open, with the bedrooms looking down from a second floor through windows to the living area below.

In the morning we were called early to watch deer walking down to drink at a stream, right next to the kitchen window. It was a magical place.

On the way back we called into this Island that Hagar had mentioned. 'You pronounce it 'Mackinow': I guess it is an Indian name.'

Despite the absence of many vehicles. . .those that we saw were Land Rover-type. . .we did not find the island reminded us of Sark. It was much flatter and the horses pulled drays in a twosome. We enjoyed the visit, and were very grateful for the effort our friends had made but it was the end of season and everything had the feeling of closing down for the long winter.

It was a wonderful holiday and introduction to the way of life in America. We ate mostly at 'Fast-food' outlets, of which there were very many, although I drew the line at 'McDonalds.' I just did not fancy the plastic-looking hamburgers. In all the places we ate we were amazed at the huge portions and learned to order from the back of the menu for 'Children and Seniors:' even so we became used to being offered 'extras' like 'biscuits'(sort of scones); salad and ice-cream.

Finally it was time to return to Sark.

'Can't wait to get home.' As usual Peter was like an excited child once we were on the Sark boat.

'You'll feel better once you are home, but you really should have a check-up. You never know what's cooking.' However, as he felt much better Peter put things off.

The days grew into weeks and we settled into winter and Christmas and before we knew it the Millennium was only a year away. We had decided to visit New Zealand again early in the year 2000, after enjoying all the celebrations planned on Sark. I was sad that I would not be seeing Roy and Annette as they had moved to Sweden some years previously. They were studying at the University in Lund for their 'Doctorates;' Roy in Computer Sciences and Annette in Geography. They were a very bright couple, and after both getting BA and MA degrees were offered the chance to study in Sweden.

In the meantime, my nursing and Homeopathic work continued. My clinic in Guernsey had grown and I had moved my rooms from the piano shop. For a little while I shared with other complementary practitioners, in an out-of-town area, but then I had the chance to use s suite of rooms right in the centre of St Peter Port. One of my patients attended a newly-set-up 'Family Planning Clinic.'

'They don't open every day, and need as much income for the rent as they can get: why don't you ask if you can set up there for one of the free days?'

I did and soon had a regular clinic on Wednesdays for a reasonable rent. I had a room to myself, a waiting room, use of a small kitchen and a toilet. It was ideal. I had become quite adept at diagnosis, and had several very successful outcomes. Whole families came to be treated, and became friends as well, for many years.

My nursing on the Island remained varied, from cutting an old lady's toe nails to caring for one of the Island's 'Characters' after she retired from running one of the hotels. Maggie had a slight stroke, brought on no doubt by a lifetime of sampling the contents of her well-stocked bar. She loved men and generally just tolerated women, but we had always got on pretty well. This was possibly because I stood up to her. Peter and I were sometimes invited as guests to dine at her hotel, although we were never quite sure what to expect. More than once we were met in the bar by her comment:

'Guess what; the bloody chef's walked out on me again.' Maggie would then proceed to cook the meal for the guests and depending on how sober she was, it was a memorable occasion in one way or another.

Eventually Maggie moved to a small bungalow, taking her large unpleasant dog with her. I agreed to call in twice a week to help her shower, and attend to her personal needs. The problem was getting her out of bed. The dog slept on it with Maggie, and each time I approached it bared its teeth and snarled at me.

'Here give the old bugger a biscuit.' I usually managed to remove him then, but my troubles were not over. Maggie was quite lonely and insisted I stay a while and have a drink with her. Coffee would have been welcome, but I drew the line at a large tumbler of whiskey at eleven in the morning. I learned to divert Maggie's attention while I tipped most down the sink and filled the glass with cold tea or coffee.

'Chris,' she said one day, 'I am worried if I get ill in the night. I've arranged to have a St John emergency call thing: will you be on my call list?' Not thinking, I agreed.

At three the next morning I was roused by the phone ringing: it was the St John emergency service.

'We've just had a call from Mrs Maggie Shaw; she says she has fallen and can't get up. Can you go round?'

Wearily I got my bike out and peddled towards Maggie's bungalow. As I approached I could see the old lady standing peering through the window. She then disappeared from sight as I opened her gate. Sure enough she was lying on the lounge floor looking upset as I entered her lounge.

I was not feeling very charitable: 'Maggie, for goodness sake I saw you at the window. What are you playing at?' I hauled her up none too gently and sat her on the settee.

'Well I just wanted to see if it worked.'

'Well it blinking well did.'

After that I persuaded David to be on the list as his farmhouse was quite near.

The Farmhouse

29

The new century began well on Sark, with public feasting and celebrations and we were soon packing and off again to New Zealand. We toured around and visited Peter's relatives: stayed with Ken and Mary: and visited all our favourite places, but I could see that Peter was slower walking and still complained of sinus trouble.

'The blessed air conditioning on the plane just doesn't suit me.' But I was a little worried: I had to remind myself that he was now 70 years old, but the brightness had dimmed.

'You are going to have a good check-up when we get home: no putting it off this time.'

As before, Peter seemed a little better when we were back on Sark, and he did not go to see the doctor straight away. He could be pretty stubborn at times.

'I'll go when Mitch comes back from his cruise; don't like that new locum.'

Quite suddenly things got worse. For anyone else I would have noticed earlier, but when you are close to someone you love, it is hard to see the signs. He started to veer to one side when we went for a walk and tired easily, but it was not until Peter kept dropping his fork while eating I realised there was something very wrong.

I took him to see the locum: but not knowing Peter, he said he would wait and see, and send him in a few days to Guernsey if he was no better. In a couple of days he was worse, and so I phoned the doctor to call as Peter was unable to walk to the surgery.

'Mmm: I think you must go over today and have a scan. I'll order the ambulance.' The doctor said little but I suspected TIAs (Transitional Ischaemic Attacks), which would account for the symptoms.

I was not prepared for the comments of the specialist in Guernsey, after the scan.

'I am sorry Mrs Curtis: there is a shadow in the left frontal lobe. I don't like the look of it: you will have to go to Southampton as soon as possible.' I still did not realise the significance of what was being said. I suppose my mind would not accept the possibility of a growth.

We booked into a hotel in Guernsey and spent an unreal evening of luxury. Peter seemed completely calm and unconcerned: child-like almost. I was just stunned at the speed of the change in our lives.

I had packed a small case for both of us, expecting just one night away, but in the event, it was several days of nightmare before we returned to Sark.

I remember little of the flight to Southampton and the taxi ride to the hospital. Peter was expected and admitted to a small side-room in a busy general ward. He showed a little of his old spark when he insisted he had health insurance and expected private treatment. I had at last realised the seriousness and phoned his daughter Lyn, who was very close to her father.

'Chris, I'll come right away.' She arrived on the day they decided to operate on Peter and do a biopsy.

I am not sure if the surgeon was annoyed at Peter's attitude, was over-worked, or just insensitive, but I will never forgive him for the way he gave us the devastating news after the operation.

In the centre of the busy ward he just announced to Lyn and myself:

'The biopsy showed that Mr Curtis has an advanced astrocytoma. It is inoperable; we removed some fluid which will give temporary relief, but it is terminal. A few months: maybe a year.'

I felt as if my brain would burst; the world stood still for a moment and I had to support myself on the wall as dizziness overtook me.

Lyn looked as stunned as I felt.

A passing nurse must have seen our distress and held my elbow. 'Are you alright, Mrs Curtis?' Anger took over.

'No of course I am not alright. I've just been told the man I love may die in a few months. Your surgeon is the most insensitive doctor I have ever met. . .and I've worked with a few.'

Lyn was recovering a little; as a social worker she was a sensible and practical woman. 'We want to talk to the surgeon again: now.'

As we went towards Peter's ward we agreed to say nothing to him. 'Maybe there is something that can be done?'

The nurse must have spoken to the doctor and said how distressed we were, as he arrived in Peter's ward soon after we did. Peter was still sleepy from the operation and was oblivious of all round him.

The surgeon took us into the nurses' office this time; he was a little contrite at his earlier insensitivity. 'I thought you would have realised what the diagnosis was likely to be as you are a nurse. I am sorry if it was a shock. I assumed they had told you in Guernsey.'

'No: but surely something can be done?'

'An operation to remove it is impossible as it is well attached to the brain. . .maybe radiotherapy may delay things a bit. I'll get in touch with Dr Wells, head of radiotherapy.'

With that we had to be content. We were still suffering from shock. I realised I should have suspected some brain problem: the constant ache to Peter's face: his tingling hand: some unusual behaviour over the past year or so, such as repeating certain words and being unconcerned about problems in his work that would normally have annoyed him. As I had said to Lyn, it is difficult to see when you are so close to someone you love.

Dispassionately I realised I was going through the stages of grief as described by Doctor Kubler-Ross that I had observed so many times in families of terminal patients: denial: anger: bargaining: depression and acceptance. I was determined not to accept that there was nothing that could be done.

Dr Wells arrived later that day and took us to a quiet place. He was the opposite in behaviour to his colleague.

'First let me say how sorry that you have had this news; but as far as. . .Peter, is it. . .is concerned, he will not suffer. I will say that if I was told I was going to have cancer, it is the one that I would choose. No pain, just gradually slipping away, and not really knowing what was happening.'

'Surely there is something to be done?'

'Well, yes, I think we could try making a mould to isolate the area in the right temporal region where the tumour is, and zapping it with radio waves. I'll prescribe some steroids to try and reduce the collection of fluid. You are a nurse, I believe Mrs Curtis?'

I nodded, unable to trust my voice.

'We will put him on a highish dose and then reduce it in stages. You will know what to look for while he is on the treatment.'

I had to ask the inevitable question.

'How long have we got?'

'It is never sure: maybe six months: if you are lucky and he responds, maybe two years, but it is pretty advanced.'

'Does that mean he has had it there for a long time?'

'Probably for years: but it would have made no difference to the outcome had it been diagnosed earlier, as it is inoperable. Sometimes these growths just sit there till the person dies naturally: sometimes something triggers it to start growing.'

I thought back to our time together, totally unsuspecting that this thing had been sitting there in Peter's brain like an alien implant. I wondered how we would have felt had we known it was there: waiting to discover if it would grow or not.

We discussed the treatment, and in the practicalities I buried my grief.

'It will be a three-month treatment: about a half to one hour each weekday. Peter will need to come in and have a plaster mould made of his head, and then as soon as we make the mask we can start at the hospital here.'

'So we will need to be here in Southampton for three months?'

'Yes I'm afraid so: do you have anyone here?'

Lyn said she knew someone who may help and so we discussed the details, as if we were planning a long holiday.

It was decided to tell Peter what was going to happen. Dr Wells was wonderful and explained to him the severity, but gave a little hope for some short-term success. Peter seemed to accept the situation: but then he had changed from the man I knew. The vitality had totally gone and in its place was a child-like acceptance.

Dr Wells said he would book us for the months of May to July. It was now the end of March and we were to return to Sark until Peter was called for a few days in a ward, to prepare him. I had to find somewhere to stay for three months: book a hire car for that time, and make arrangements for our cats and home to be looked after: and tell the rest of our families and friends. I was going to need all the strength I could muster. My arrow-prayers were sent quickly and frequently.

30

After steroids started to reduce the fluid which filled the centre of the tumour and the pressure was lessened, I could almost believe the old Peter was returning. The trip home from Southampton was easy and we talked about the future.

'We need to find somewhere to stay for three months. We can make a holiday of it and drive around to explore the New Forest.' I was not sure if Peter was in denial, or really believed he would be cured: but I played along with it. After all Dr Wells had said we might have another two years.

The month before we were due to return to Southampton was busy with plans. People had to be told. In a place like this tiny Island, speculation would be rife and it was easier for the truth to be told. It was hard at first, and it was only with my closest friends that I broke down and spoke of the prognosis.

True to her word, Lyn put us in touch with someone who let out a couple of cottages in a village not far from the hospital in Southampton.

'You'll have to change from one to the other a bit, and I'm afraid there are two weeks at the end of June where they are full. Maybe you can find somewhere near the harbour.'

I was relieved to have that problem solved, and contacted a car-hire firm that we had used before. They gave us a very good rate for three months hire. For a while it was almost like planning a holiday, except that Peter usually did the bookings and now he left it all to me.

The cottages were thatched and well equipped and under any other circumstance, I would have enjoyed the lovely location in a friendly village. For the middle two weeks we managed to rent a flat overlooking the Yacht Marina.

We fell into a routine: a lazy morning: a trip to the hospital for Peter's treatment at twelve noon which only took an hour, and then a drive around the country to explore this beautiful part of southern England. It was spring and blossoms showed pink and white in every garden. I renewed my acquaintance with the stately New Forest now bursting with bright green leaves. My family had lived in a suburb of Southampton when my father had been a customs officer and we had often taken trips out by bicycle to explore the area.

Now Peter and I toured round by car in the best of English weather, trying to ignore the black cloud that was always hovering near. I could almost believe the treatment was working, but realised I was fooling myself. Though slower and more pedantic, Peter appeared almost normal: except for some odd behaviour. I made the mistake of letting him map-read at first, until I realized he was just giving random directions, as a child would. He so wanted to help that I let him do several little jobs: one at the end of our stay was to fill up the windscreen-washer water container. It was not until our bill for the hire car was sent, that I realized he had topped up the brake fluid container with water, necessitating the whole system to be drained. We were lucky to avoid a serious accident. I realised then that I was on my own and would have to make all the decisions.

For about four months after we returned to Sark, the radiotherapy appeared to have helped. I was instructed to juggle the steroids, depending on Peter's condition, but they had the effect of causing Peter to put on so much weight that he looked like a benign Buddha.

We tried to live as normal a life as we could, but gradually we had to resort to a wheelchair. For the first time I regretted the absence of cars on Sark. It would have been so much easier to drive around instead of having to push a wheelchair over stony roads.

I tried to take Peter to as many things as we could together: church: friends' houses: public occasions like the church fete, and even to have a meal at our favourite hotel. The owners, who were friends, suggested we use a convenient ground-floor room and stay overnight.

Once or twice we went over to Guernsey, as I tried to keep my clinic going, having held phone consultations while we were in Southampton. It was impossible for Peter to walk around, but we managed once or twice. Gradually it became more difficult, and I arranged for a friend to stay as a companion in Sark while I went on my own to the neighbouring island. Peter was not happy about that. His possessiveness had increased with his dependence and after one unpleasant occasion, I had to abandon my trips.

When I returned from this particular clinic, I discovered the friend fast asleep in the lounge. Peter was not with him and so I went to the bedroom. I knew he could walk around the house by supporting himself on the walls but was not prepared for what I discovered. Peter was lying half in and half out of the bathroom, with no lower garments: the bathroom was awash with urine. As I ran towards him I noticed that there was a pillow from the bed under Peter's head. It was only later I realised that it could not have been put there by our babysitting friend.

'Are you alright my darling? I'll not leave you again.'

'No you'd better not. I might hurt myself next time.'

I knew I was being manipulated, but I also knew we did not have much more time together and it was a small price to pay.

The falls became frequent, and I was fortunate to be able to buy a mechanical seat. It was mainly for use in a bath, but I could get Peter to wriggle onto it and pump it up until he could stand again.

We had had a spa bath installed and Peter loved to be lowered into it, however it became difficult to get him out. One time he got in, being lowered by the seat, but he then slipped off and I just could not get him to wriggle back onto it to winch him out. I realised I would have to get in with Peter, to help him. I stripped off and we managed together. As I was drying him, a flash of the old Peter showed as he chuckled, 'Not many nurses would get in the bath with their patients!' The times were few and far between that I would see my dear friend and lover again. The strain was sometimes too much, and I had to let off the steam of frustration. Once when I was in the kitchen I could feel it boiling up and let out a scream and yelled; 'I can't stand it!'

A little later when I was with Peter he said, 'What was that noise I heard?'

'Oh, er, I trod on the cat's tail.'

Most of the time, I had to accept that the tumour had made Peter return to a dependant childhood. It made me sympathise with people who looked after sufferers of Alzheimer's dementia. The falls were sudden and frequent but we managed to get out and about on fine days, using the wheelchair. There were sometimes a few problems when we were in public if he wanted to go to the toilet, as happened in church one Sunday, he would just start to pull his trousers down.

I became adept at getting him onto the wheelchair and to the nearest 'Gents', just hoping no-one else came in.

Night-time was a problem too, as Peter seemed unable to turn over. As a district nurse, I had learned to fold a sheet in half across the bed, under the patient, leaving a length at one side of the bed: it was then quite easy to cross one of the patient's ankles over the other and pull the sheet through, with the patient on it and flip him over. I was worried about bedsores and had to do this several times a night.

When I was a district nurse looking after terminal patients, I had often been surprised that the partner of the very ill patient still slept in the same double bed. I now realised how important that is for both people. However ill a person is, contact is vital and I now know from my experience that comfort and strength can come from it.

31

The months passed and December approached. We were due to return to the Southampton hospital to be assessed early in that month. My 60th birthday was due on the first of December, but I had not expected any celebrations. Still showing a few surprises, Peter suddenly announced.

'I would like to give you a big party for your birthday, and I want you to go to Guernsey and buy a nice party frock.' He shakily wrote a generous cheque as I tried to hide my tears. How I still loved this guy.

The trip to Guernsey in itself was a treat, and friends looked after Peter for the day. I chose a lovely silky suit with snug-fitting jacket, long skirt and trousers to match in a gold colour. I even had time to see a few patients at my clinic.

When I dressed up to show Peter, he seemed a little disappointed.

'I thought you would get a nice frilly frock. . .but if you like it. . .'

We invited about 30 friends to our favourite hotel, and they put on a wonderful buffet: we stayed the night. Both my brother David from Holland and Roy from Sweden came over too, which was wonderful. It was a bitter-sweet occasion, as we all knew it would probably be a 'good-bye' party for Peter too, but he raised himself for the occasion. I never really knew if he realised how ill he was: if the apparent return to childhood was genuine, or a defence against reality.

Peter's daughter Lyn and family had moved to a new house: a converted chapel, and Peter said he wanted to go there for Christmas. I was not sure if he was well enough but was happy that he showed some interest. We agreed we would return to Sark after his Hospital appointment and then go up to Lyn a few days before the holiday. Sadly it was not to work out like that.

After the party Peter seemed more confused, and it was with difficulty we managed to reach Southampton. I had to arrange to have a carry-on seat to get him down the steep steps at the Sark harbour, and the boat crew were wonderful in steering to a ramp in Guernsey where the taxi could get to the water's edge. I took a wheelchair with me and we made the rest of the journey with considerable help from the airline staff.

We had some wonderful friends who lived in Southampton and they insisted we stay while attending the follow-up appointment. I shall never forget the generosity and selflessness of my friend. Some time after our stay, she confided in me that she had had a diagnosis of breast cancer while we were staying with her. She said nothing to me at the time, but later said that my problems took the worry from her concern about herself.

I knew Peter was getting worse: my fear that the tumour had grown again were confirmed by Dr Wells after he had made his examination. He took us both into his office and gave us the bad news.

'I am sorry, Mr Curtis, there is nothing else we can do.'

'You can operate again: give some more radiotherapy? There must be something!' For the first time Peter was shaken from his apparent acceptance. I realised then that he really had convinced himself that he might get better.

From that moment Peter's fight went and he seemed to have no interest in anything. I decided it would be best to go straight to his daughter, rather than both go back to Sark first as planned.

'The doctor said you can stay in the hospital a few days and they will sort your steroids out. I will go back to Sark and get all the Christmas presents and collect you. Then we'll go up to Lyn's. OK?'

I was not sure if Peter had understood, and it was with a heavy heart I returned to Sark. Unfortunately the weather turned wild, and the boats were cancelled for a couple of days. It was a week before I returned to the Hospital. What I found broke my heart.

'Mr Curtis seemed to think you had left him here. He has been so difficult. Won't eat, and we had to put a catheter in as he was wetting the bed.'

My poor Peter was in quite a state and it took me hours to convince him that he had not been abandoned. I realised that he was in no shape to do other than return to Sark with me.

'You'll never manage on your own.'

'Of course I will: it is what I have been doing for years. It's a poor thing if I can't do it for the man I love.'

I phoned the St John ambulance equipment loan department in Guernsey. I tried to be business-like. I could not cope with sympathy at this time: there was too much to organise.

'I need a hoist; hospital bed; commode and a ripple mattress, please.' I gave my address and was relieved that they could all be delivered a day before we would return to Sark. I was not sure how I would get everything set up, but I decided to think about that later. In the meantime I had to arrange an ambulance from the hospital to the Southampton airport: an ambulance from Guernsey airport to the Sark boat: help to carry Peter onto the boat and the Sark ambulance at the other end. He had deteriorated so much that all this was now necessary. I decided to ask my friends on the Sark Ambulance to help me set everything up, but in the event it was not necessary.

Everything went like clockwork. The ambulance people were wonderful, driving right to the plane and carrying Peter on and off by a carry-seat.

I had phoned David and Hilly to tell them we were returning, and what had happened. Bless them, they had assembled all the equipment: put the heating on and even put a vase of flowers in our bedroom for when we arrived.

We had a quiet Christmas. I had nothing in the house, having planned to be with Lyn, but David and Hilly brought food over.

Whether it was the advancing tumour or the fact that Peter had given up, the end came quite quickly. My days were taken up with what we nurses used to call 'heavy nursing.' Everything had to be done for Peter, from shaving, feeding, washing and the more intimate personal things. The ripple mattress, like the one I had used for Hap, helped to prevent bedsores. Thanks to the hoist I was able to get Peter up and into the lounge most days. How I blessed the advice we had been given to have wider passageways when planning the building.

The family visited regularly, as did our friends, and I was able to pop out for a walk or a coffee occasionally. Towards the middle of January, 2001 I had made such a plan to have lunch with a friend. Two others were coming in to sit with Peter. He had stopped eating anything but ice-cream and jelly and I knew he was slipping into a coma, but I used to put the radio on his pillow as I was sure he could hear it. On this day, an hour or so before I was due to go out I tuned into the music programme, and bent over to kiss Peter's forehead: his eyebrows flicked and there was a faint smile on his lips.

A moment later I heard the programme change to talking and went in to change it. I looked at Peter, and realised he had slipped away.

The reaction did not set in immediately. I phoned the doctor and the mechanism was put into motion that I had so often done before for others.

It was the end of an era, but somehow I had to go on living.

**'The Cottage' before
and after**

32

There was so much to attend to for the next few weeks that I did not have much time for grief. The tears would come later.

There was a funeral to arrange, and a cremation and wake in Guernsey for immediate friends and family. We decided that we should have a proper send-off in April, when relatives and friends from overseas could attend. In the event it was the sort of occasion Peter would have loved: a well-known cellist performed in the church in a lively service.

People were asked to wear bright clothes, and a large party for 200 guests was held in the hall.

Later I and the family went to Peter's favourite beach of Grande Greve to scatter his ashes. Even that had a lighter note as the wind flurried and sent his ashes scuttling, so we had to dodge to avoid getting covered with them.

'Trust Dad!' David exclaimed.

For a while I had stayed with Hilly and David, but I needed to return to Camp Farm and sort everything. A friend helped me pack Peter's clothes and after I offered David his pick, we sent everything to the Salvation Army in Guernsey. I could not bear the thought of seeing people wearing Peter's clothes in the small Sark community. As it was I was to have a few heart-stopping moments when I saw David in the distance wearing one of Peter's favourite sweaters.

The inheritance laws on Sark are still feudal. Although Camp Farm was equally owned by Peter and me, at his death the whole property reverted to me and my heirs. Knowing that Peter's family would have no claim, we had arranged that all his finance would go to his heirs. As I had little money of my own, as most had gone into the rebuild, I realised I would have to sell Camp Farm. In any case I did not feel I could live there without Peter.

The weeks of sorting, dismantling the model railway and handing it on to David, and preparing the place to put on the market, filled my days. It was the nights that seemed to last forever. The line in the old song, 'It's the wee small hours of the morning, that I miss you most,' constantly ran through my head.

I refused anti-depressants: I could still remember their effect when I had post-natal depression after having Roy. Instead I relied on homeopathy and herbal medicine and somehow I got through.

Having decided to sell, I had to find somewhere else to live. I did seriously think of moving back to New Zealand, but Roy and Annette were still in Sweden, and I felt I did not want to leave Sark just yet.

I had to find somewhere that would leave money to invest to live on, and I wanted a property that I could work on to keep me sane. Eventually I remembered visiting an old couple who lived in a 400 year old cottage, tucked away down a lane. I knew the old man had died and his wife moved in with her daughter. I also remembered that it had been cluttered to overflowing with clothes and articles from numerous jumble sales, so could not visualise how big it was inside, but it was made of granite and had a walled garden. When I walked down the lane, I hardly recognised the sad, derelict-looking cottage and was amazed at the size of the garden, now it had been cleared. The tile roof was sunken and the old stone wall by the road crumbling, but my heart lifted for the first time in months. I could see the possibilities and it was just what I needed.

The problem was that it was not for sale; or at least not on its own. The cottage was part of one of the 40 original tenements, which was for sale. I contacted the absentee owner and after much wrangling, finally bought a reasonably-sized lease for more than it was worth. I had to borrow from the bank, but fortunately Camp Farm sold quite quickly. I was able to stay in the house for a few months while I started renovations on the cottage.

I had grown up with parents who liked to renovate old properties, and I had learned from them. I had a good builder who had rebuilt Camp Farm and he was happy to discuss plans with me, and in no time work began. The roof had to go but I salvaged the old beams which had been boxed in.

'These will be really old: I would say they came from a wrecked ship.' The builder pointed to some holes that had possibly had plugs in place, once.

The more recent addition of a kitchen, we thought in Victorian times, was pulled down and the excellent granite used to face a wall in a new extension. The old building was gutted and became a large kitchen/dining room.

I was determined to have a Rayburn, and that was set in the old fireplace. A mirror that had been left, after I repainted the frame, was hung back in its old place. Soon the older part had an upstairs lounge, with dormer windows. The newer part, built at right-angles housed an en-suite flat that I intended to let as self-catering, and a laundry. Upstairs was my en-suite bedroom.

As there was strict control about height, we had to keep to the original roof-line, so all the upstairs rooms had restricted head-room at the sides.

Time and money were running out. I was relying on interest on capital to finance the finishing, so had to wait until it accumulated. It was approaching time to leave Camp Farm and the plumber had not completed his work: the walls had to be plastered and there were no internal doors, let alone skirting boards and architraves. I had to tell the builder that as soon as it was possible to move in I would, and would do the finishing myself. A very good friend who was a wonderful handyman agreed to do the heavier stuff, bit by bit as I could afford it, and I intended to do all the decorating, and fancied trying my hand at some of the woodwork.

I asked the builder how much longer before I could move in.

'Well I guess about a month. You can move your furniture into the kitchen and spare room, but the water from the borehole isn't connected and the toilets need to be piped to the septic tank.'

A couple of wonderful friends came to my rescue for part of the time between moving out of Camp Farm and into the cottage. They had a modernised house that Peter and I had visited many times for meals.

'Why don't you come and house-sit for the two weeks we are away on a cruise? You can look after the cat and keep the Aga going.'

So I packed up my furniture and most of my clothes and my local carter ferried it all to my new cottage. Food and my immediate needs I stowed in my wheelbarrow and trundled down the road to my friends' house. I spent the time decorating my bedroom and the upstairs lounge, returning late to a warm house and a welcoming cat. I did not bother much with food: I was too tired.

I was concerned about the final two weeks, but need not have worried. Another good friend, a feisty elderly lady I had befriended in the church choir, insisted I move in with her for the rest of the time. So I packed up my wheelbarrow again, and like a homeless bag-lady set off for my new accommodation, which was just down the road from my cottage. She was a real friend in need. After a tiring day of decorating and sorting furniture in a cold place, I would stagger to my friend's house, to find a hot bath, a large whiskey and a lovely meal waiting for me.

Finally, I could move into my unfinished house, and suddenly I felt very much on my own. After all the excitement and activity I realised I did not know what I was going to do with the rest of my life. This was when the real grieving started, and it was to have a long-term effect on my health.

For several weeks I had had cramping gut pain and spending too much time in the toilet. Food just passed through, leaving me weak and sore. I realised I would have to go to the doctor.

'It may be nothing; grieving does that, as you know, but I think you should have some tests.'

Another trip to a hospital: fortunately just Guernsey this time. After some unpleasant examinations I was told I had colitis.

'We'll try you on steroids for a month and see how you get on.'

'If it is all the same to you, doctor, I would rather try my way first.' I was determined to avoid them if I could.

I did manage to control the problem most of the time with herbal medicine and homeopathy, but some foods still can cause an upset. I just had to learn to live with it.

'The Cottage'

33

I moved into 'The Cottage' in the summer of 2001. There was so much to do that I was grateful, as it kept my mind occupied. I borrowed a useful little device called a 'Mitre Block', to get the angles right in the architraves round the doorways. I am fortunately pretty handy and soon got the hang of it: at least downstairs where the doors were standard. Upstairs it was a different story. As the doors to my bedroom and the lounge were set in the roof angle; they were not standard. I had to custom-cut to make them fit and did not do such a good job. My odd-job-builder friend, who was a perfectionist, remarked that they looked 'a little rustic.'

My friend made all the doors in a panelled 'cottage-style' with black metal latches. I stained the doors, the architraves and skirting in an antique pine varnish and they fitted in well with the cottage theme. There were yards and yards of skirting to stain, cut to size and glue into place, but it occupied me through the long lonely evenings, when the light was not so good for painting the walls. Night after night I tumbled into bed, sometimes too tired to bother to undress properly.

There were one or two lighter moments, like the evening I decided to stain the narrow stairs that ran from the hall downstairs to the upper floor. Like a fool I started at the top and then realised I needed to go upstairs to bed, but of course the varnish was still wet. I had the bright idea of treading on the brushes I had just used to varnish, one at a time, step by step. I would have to sandpaper the dried steps anyway before the next coat, so could remove any marks later. I was progressing well and congratulated myself, when I got to the bend. Pride, they say, comes before a fall and I suddenly found myself sliding backwards, sitting heavily on one sticky step, with both hands on the lower one. It was the first time I had laughed in a long time.

The garden was another challenge. My mother had been an expert gardener, and I had been keen to learn from her. We had moved house frequently, and Phyl delighted in redesigning each garden. She would have delighted in the 'blank pallet' at 'The Cottage' and I put into practice what she had taught me. I first drew a scale plan and sketched the location of beds, paths and lawn. It was an odd, almost kite-shaped piece of land, with the cottage placed at one corner boundary, by the access lane. A tumble-down dry-stone wall ran along the side of the lane and joined a high stone wall which separated me from my neighbour. At the back was another dry-stone wall, and a tangled copse of old trees entwined with brambles. For the rest, the garden looked like a building site, which it had been. I never understood why the builders had felt it necessary to mix their concrete in several different places, resulting in a sold area in front of the cottage.

Eventually I established a path of large paving stones, pick axing my way through the layers and laying the stones on sand.

The rest of the area in front I scattered with gravel, and made the most of the fact that weeds could not grow through the concrete.

The soil had been neglected for so long that I found it necessary to buy two trailer-loads of topsoil. An old cafe was being extended and the soil came from this, but unfortunately it was peppered with old pieces of broken glass and crockery. These had to be removed before I could shovel it to the areas where I had decided to plant my flower beds. By the time I had done this, I still had a rounded mound in the middle of the garden and decided I would leave it like that and make a novelty lawn. It became quite a talking point by visitors in the years to come, though I did find mowing it a challenge.

Gradually the garden took shape. I had dug up my favourite roses from Camp Farm before it was sold, and had taken numerous cuttings. I was particularly proud of a third-generation rosemary bush I grew from a cutting of a bush that had been in my mother's garden.

There were many small pieces of granite left from the building and I used them for border edges. I planted a vegetable garden: encouraged a wild area where there had been a pile of rubble, and established a rock garden and buried an old bath to make a pond. I then turned to the woodland behind the cottage. I knew that the cliff and sea were beyond and had visions of making an access by climbing over the back wall and hacking down the brambles till I could see the sea.

It was not to be that easy. I discovered that previous residents had enjoyed their drink and had disposed of the bottles by throwing them over the back wall. Judging by the quantity this had been going on for a couple of centuries. Eventually I disposed of several containers-full and packed some old strips of carpet on top of the remaining piles, to make a safe pathway. By sheer determination I gradually battled my way through to a sea view, but it never became the attractive area I had planned.

This copse belonged to the 'Tenement', as did the farm buildings to the other side of my property and another derelict cottage across the lane. The main house was also on the opposite side, and had a huge garden. I had visited that house some years ago and still cringed at my experience there.

The Tenement had been owned by a wealthy lady, belonging to one of the English titled families. She was well known to Peter through music contacts and he called her by her Christian name, if we should mention her in our conversation, so I always thought of her in that way.

A friend had broken her ankle and this charitable lady offered her a room and the help of her servants for a few days. I phoned and enquired after my friend and was invited to tea.

I was ushered into the lounge, and was happy to see my friend looking relaxed, and turned to my hostess.

'It is so kind of you. . .may I call you Valerie?'

The aristocratic elderly lady looked me up and down, and in the best upper-class accents said,

'I really don't think we know each other well enough for *that,* do we Mrs Curtis?'

If there had been a hole, I would gladly have crawled into it.

Now the lady was dead and it was her nephew that was selling the large property of which my cottage was a part. I had been a little concerned when I arranged my lease: I had never had a rented or leased property before and wondered how much control a new owner would have over my day-to-day life. I need not have worried. Not long after I moved in David called to see me.

'How would you feel about having me as your landlord?'

I knew he had wanted to have a freehold property, and it transpired that he had worked out how to own this one. I was delighted. There was an enormous amount to be done to the main house, but he was a very competent handyman and apparently someone had shown an interest in buying a lease on the other old cottage.

My new life was taking shape. I had kept active in the Sark Garden Walks as much as I could during Peter's illness. Now I threw myself into its organisation and took on the presidency; the other two organisers had stepped back due to illness and other calls on their time. It was mostly on my shoulders now. People came back at the same time of year and looked on the weekly walk as a necessary part of their holiday. I welcomed some visitors as old friends and was happy to include my new developing garden and cottage in the 'Tea-stop' places. They used to say such things as;

'Oh I see you have put a rose-arch up. What happened to that tree?'

I was happy to show off my little cottage too, and had several people returning to rent the self-catering flat.

It was also good to have Peter's family so close. David used the sheds behind my cottage for storing equipment and mounds of potatoes, and I saw him most days. The 'children,' now growing up fast, dropped in and at Christmas still settled down together to watch 'The Muppets' Christmas,' with a glass of weak wine instead of hot chocolate.

'What you need,' Pippa said one day, 'is a cat. I know where there is a litter of kittens in Little Sark.'

So that was how 'Mischief' came into my life.

When I knelt among the frolicking bundles of fluff, a strikingly handsome little tabby wandered over and curled up on my knee. It was love at first sight.

'You have a bit of a problem here, Chris;' my vet friend said as I asked him to check my little fellow's health, 'he is nearly blind; he's got congenital cataracts. Look you can see he is cross-eyed.'

That made me love my little cat even more. He had the sweetest nature, although he was always getting into trouble with other cats in the neighbourhood. I think he just did not see how big and ferocious they were. He was more like a dog, following me around: even when I went into the woodland behind to work, he was not far away.

There are moments that remain with you the rest on your life. One warm spring day a few years after Peter's death, I was sitting on a comfortable rocking chair just inside my kitchen with the door wide open and the sunlight streaming in. Mischief was on my knee, purring as I stroked him. A blackbird started to sing and a waft of perfume from the roses by the door blew in on the breeze.

A line of Robert Browning came into my head: 'God's in His Heaven, and all's right with the world.'

'Maybe not quite right yet,' I whispered to Mischief, 'but getting there.'

****

EPILOGUE

I stayed on Sark until 2009, nursing and running my 'Healthy Life Clinic' but then everything changed.

Roy and family moved back to New Zealand, and as there had been a financial crisis with the British Pound, my income from investments was greatly reduced.

I could not afford to remain on the Island, and anyway I felt it was time to move.

David and I made an arrangement for him to buy back the Cottage, and I packed up my life, travelling out once more to New Zealand, where I now will live for the rest of my life.

But I left a little on my heart in that strange, unique little Island.